On Sunday Morning She Gathered Herbs

Ol'ha Kobylians'ka

On Sunday Morning She Gathered Herbs

Translated by Mary Skrypnyk

With an introduction by
Maxim Tarnawsky

Canadian Institute of Ukrainian Studies Press
Edmonton   2001   Toronto

Canadian Institute of Ukrainian Studies Press
University of Alberta   University of Toronto
Edmonton, Alberta   Toronto, Ontario
T6G 2E8 CANADA   M5S 1A1 CANADA

Canadian Cataloguing in Publication Data

Kobylians'ka, Ol'ha 1863–1942
    On sunday morning she gathered herbs

Translation of: V nediliu rano zilie kopala.
ISBN 1–895571–34–0

I. Skrypnyk, Mary, 1917–   . II. Title

PG39480.K35V513 2000 . 891.7'933   C00-930735-4

Printed in Canada

The Duality of Ol'ha Kobylians'ka

Judging by the available evidence, Ol'ha Kobylians'ka was at least two persons. Among those familiar with her works, she has a reputation as a defender of the Ukrainian common man, a devoted student of the culture of the Ukrainian peasantry, and a storyteller for whom the plight of the poor and the neglected was a particular concern. Yet, among these same readers, she is also known for her bold iconoclastic views, for her feminist inclinations and, above all, for her intense dedication to the pursuit of the lofty and the beautiful and aversion to everything common and ugly.

Kobylians'ka's attraction to the world of the Ukrainian peasants is richly evident in her works. That a woman educated in a German-speaking environment, who attended a German elementary school and who wrote her first literary works in that language, made the effort to learn Ukrainian well enough to write fiction already speaks volumes about her attachment to the culture of her nation. At the end of the nineteenth century Ukrainian culture was still primarily (albeit with some very important exceptions) concerned with and dedicated to the Ukrainian peasant, who constituted the overwhelming mass of the Ukrainian population. Choosing to write in Ukrainian rather than German was to a certain degree a choice in favor of provinciality and the lower classes, over the refined culture of the European upper classes. Kobylians'ka's choice is further evidenced in the setting of many of her works. One of her best-known works, the novel *Zemlia* (The Land) is, as its title suggests, a study of peasant life. The present text, *V nediliu rano zillia kopala (On Sunday Morning She Gathered Herbs)*, is not only a novel about simple village folk, but a work derived from a very well-known Ukrainian folk song.

At the same time, however, Kobylians'ka is not quite a populist admirer of the common village. Indeed, one of the most respected populist literary critics of the day, Serhii Iefremov, who admired all things connected to Ukrainian village folk, greeted Kobylians'ka's early works with scorn. For

him, Kobylians'ka's feminist views, her unmistakable debt to Nietzsche, and
her focus on the individual and the individual's aspirations to rise above the
common rank of humanity were not compatible with a populist agenda. In
Iefremov's eyes, Kobylians'ka was clearly a modernist—a "decadent" writer.
Indeed, any reader of Kobylians'ka's work cannot help but observe that the
protagonists of her works are always struggling to escape the common and the
mundane. In particular, Natalka Verkovychivna, the proud orphan of
Kobylians'ka's 1895 novel, *Tsarivna* (The Princess), exemplifies the ideal of
an eternal quest for spiritual, intellectual, and aesthetic ennoblement. This
"aristocratic" stance, as it was often called by contemporary critics, placed
Kobylians'ka squarely in the camp of the young innovators who were guiding
Ukrainian literature away from the old platitudes of populist realism. "I was
often obliged in my life to struggle with narrow-mindedness, dull-wittedness,
and servile views which derived from traditional crustiness and through their
longevity had become strong," says Kobylians'ka in her 1927 autobiographical
essay.[1] The crust of tradition that many of her characters endeavor to escape
is found in many places: in the materialism of both the petty bourgeoisie and
the peasants, in the self-righteousness of the liberal intelligentsia, in the
narrow-mindedness of provincial society, in the discrimination with which
families and society treat women, and in the fear of their own limitations that
individuals harbor in the depths of their own hearts. It can also be found in
the fictionalized folk song characters of this work, *On Sunday Morning She
Gathered Herbs*.

In her 1903 autobiography, Kobylians'ka mentions her acquaintance with
the Bulgarian writer Petko Todorov (1879–1916), known particularly for his
treatment of folk themes in literature. "This young artist has influenced me so
very strongly with his new, thoroughly original, and very valuable views on
literature and art that I want to abandon the old path of literary modernism,
which I was following, and to turn onto his path, which seems to me the
proper and only path for preserving the true art and poetry of the folk, the
folk character, unchanged by hyper-culture, but conveyed solely through the
prism of fresh talent, like folk poetry dressed in melodies, for the whole world
to admire its folk treasures, heretofore barely noticed."[2] Although the degree
to which Kobylians'ka abandoned modernist techniques is debatable, the
earlier works in her oeuvre are clearly somewhat different from the later ones.

---

1. Ol'ha Kobylians'ka, *Tvory v p'iaty tomakh* (Kyiv, 1963), vol. 5, p. 223.
2. Ibid., p. 217.

But the difference between her earlier and her later works is not merely a matter of turning explicitly to folklore, since it is only in this novel that Kobylians'ka makes such an attempt.

Over the years the popular Ukrainian folk song "Oi ne khody Hrytsiu ..." has attracted a number of writers. The tragic story of a young man torn between two women and poisoned by one of them lends itself readily to melodramatic literary interpretations. It has been set to music, dramatized on the stage, and treated in historical epics. Among the various incarnations of this story, Kobylians'ka's novel stands out for the originality of its treatment and the breadth of its thematic scope. Although Kobylians'ka may not have been aware of some of the earlier literary treatments of this folk song, no doubt she was mindful of the novelty of the motifs she was introducing.

Fictionalizing a popular story is, of necessity, a confining task. Kobylians'ka emphatically embraces these limits by including the text of the original folk song as an epigraph to her short novel. But the story line sketched out in the song leaves much to the imagination, specifically, the personalities of the central characters in the drama. Traditional readings suggest that the dark-haired poisoner is a faithful but uninspiring companion while the "other woman" is the irresistible seductress. Hryts is generally seen as an indecisive victim. The original song also requires the presence of the poisoner's mother, as a knowledgeable, chastising voice of grief and condemnation.

Kobylians'ka makes a number of distinctive additions and modifications to the basic story. The most important of these is Mavra, a character who is not presupposed by the original story but becomes, in Kobylians'ka's work, the central focus of the novel. Mavra plays a number of roles in Kobylians'ka's re-telling of the folk story. She is Hryts's mother, Tetiana's mentor, and the source of the poisonous herbs. But she is also a dramatic mirror of the central conflict in the story. She is a thematic foil to Tetiana's dilemma—another embodiment of the central conflict in the novel.

The story of Mavra's rescue from the wrath of her husband and the Gypsy community is entirely Kobylians'ka's invention—there is no such incident in the original folk song. It does much to add color and drama to the story and establishes the essential themes that Kobylians'ka sees in the folk song about Hryts's poisoning. Within her own Gypsy (Roma) community, Mavra is both a sinner and a victim. That community's strict social order does not allow for personal pleasure-seeking or mercy, particularly for women. Kobylians'ka is careful to maintain a balance between the community's justified outrage at infidelity and Mavra's relative innocence. Mavra succumbed to love, to the longing for personal happiness. Is this really a crime punishable by death? By giving Mavra's story so much attention in the novel and by treating this predicament with sympathy and understanding, Kobylians'ka encourages the reader to indulge not only a romantic sensibility regarding the fate of lovers, but also an individualistic and iconoclastic ambivalence regarding social norms and individual freedom.

Yet, despite this ambivalence, Kobylians'ka's approach also embodies a profound moral certainty. The consistent use of black and white color symbols and the scrutiny with which behavior is judged clearly demonstrate that Kobylians'ka has not abandoned traditional, particularly Christian, modes of thinking. Indeed, *On Sunday Morning She Gathered Herbs*, like her earlier *Zemlia* and *Nioba*, are, to some degree, extended meditations on Biblical subjects.

Like a prophet of the Old Testament, after the trauma of her rescue and separation from her child have subsided, Mavra chooses to lead the life of a social outcast, a loner. She moves to the shepherds' hut near the white rock on the mountain called Chabanytsia. The knowledge of herbs (a required element of the plot) that she pursues there, together with her proud disposition, give her special social standing. Moreover, in an emotional, psychological, and symbolic sense, she passes on her unique station to her spiritual ward Tetiana, who often joins her in the shepherds' hut and adopts some of her solitary, individualistic habits.

Mavra and Tetiana are unusual women. They do not fit into their surroundings. Mavra is literally a foreigner, a Gypsy among the Ukrainian villagers. Tetiana's nickname, 'Turkynia' (Turkish girl), which she acquires by wearing the half-moon earrings Mavra gave her, also marks her as something of a foreigner. They are both beautiful, proud, and resolute. Along with Tetiana's mother, the widow Ivanykha Dub, they form a threesome of remarkably independent women who see themselves as the equals of the men they encounter. Tetiana and her mother reject all her suitors in the firm conviction that she deserves someone finer than the men available in her own village. Tetiana, of course, wants to choose on the basis of love, but she is wary of the consequences of such a choice.

The decision that Tetiana must make in the novel is determined by the plot. The reader knows that Hryts also loves another girl—the folk song says so. So Kobylians'ka must choose how to depict the dilemma. The first choice Kobylians'ka makes, and it is indicative of her understanding of the story, is to make this Tetiana's dilemma, not Hryts's. Kobylians'ka gives Hryts a major role in this story, but her focus is on Tetiana and Mavra.

The author's second choice concerns the nature of the problem. This is where Kobylians'ka makes her personal sentiments apparent. Tetiana's dilemma is defined as a conflict between romance and pragmatism, between instinct and self-control, between personal happiness and social constraints, between freedom and its practical limitations. It is also, of course, a conflict between the sexes. In the novel itself, Mavra tells Tetiana how her aristocratic lover dismissed her with a whistle when she lamented her inevitable punishment. "Don't," she tells Tetiana, "love behind your mother's back and don't love two at the same time.... Be careful ... be cautious ... so you don't end up with a whistle...." From that point on, the substance of the novel is devoted to the dramatic tension created by Tetiana's interaction with Hryts. The proud girl wants to give in to the pleasure of her feelings, but without the risks. She wants to be loved, but on her own terms, without submissiveness. She loves Hryts, but she must continually test both him and herself.

Here, Kobylians'ka's task as a writer is to illustrate the inner conflict within both Tetiana and Hryts. The plot needs no attention, since the outcome is foreordained. And so, in a series of meetings between the lovers, she shows them re-enacting the same confrontation, repeating the same ideas, often with the same phrases. The repetitive nature of the writing underscores the symbolic significance of the words. These are not mere trysts between two lovers, but instances of the eternal confrontation between pride and love, freedom and comfort. Kobylians'ka's feminist inclination and autobiographical sensibility place the conflict in the hearts of two women, Tetiana and Mavra. But Hryts, too, is a captive of this same polarity. Indeed, it is he who is described in the novel as the one with a dual personality or dual soul.

This allusion to Goethe's *Faust* is not surprising, given Kobylians'ka's familiarity with German literature. The comparison between the dilemmas of Tetiana and Hryts and that of Dr. Faustus is very revealing. For Kobylians'ka, the struggle her characters endure is no less significant and no less instructive than Faust's pact with the devil. But Kobylians'ka is far less sanguine about the potential for human personal achievement. Even in her earlier, more Nietzschean works, her heroines had to effect a compromise between their ambitions and the society in which they lived. In *On Sunday Morning She Gathered Herbs* the folkloric material Kobylians'ka chooses as her base allows her to focus exclusively on the stylized presentation of the dilemma itself. It is the individual's experience of freedom's limitations that she wishes to examine, not the philosophy that explains it. The age-old folk song she selects for a plot line permits her to concentrate solely on the dramatic tension within her characters.

Ol'ha Kobylians'ka was born on 27 November 1863 in Bukovyna, then a province of the Austro-Hungarian Empire. Her birthplace, Gura Humorului, is now in Romania. The population of this corner of the Carpathian Mountains consisted of various nationalities, among which Ukrainians were quite prominent. Ol'ha's father, a Ukrainian, was a minor government official. Her mother was of Polish and German heritage. In keeping with the custom of the times in Bukovyna, Ol'ha, unlike her brothers, received only a primary education. The education she did receive was in German.

Thus Kobylians'ka was largely a self-made and self-educated writer. Her first literary attempts were in German. Under the influence of prominent Ukrainian women, such as Sofia Okunevs'ka and Nataliia Kobryns'ka, Kobylians'ka began writing in Ukrainian, at first tentatively and with some difficulty, but eventually with confidence and masterful control. Kobylians'ka was also active in the Ukrainian women's movement, where she developed close personal ties with Lesia Ukrainka, one of Ukraine's most prominent intellectual writers. Her early works, including the novels *Liudyna* (A Person, 1891) and *Tsarivna*, have as their protagonists cultured, emancipated women oppressed in a philistine, provincial society. These and other semi-autobiographical works show the influence of Friedrich Nietzsche. Her later works, particularly *Zemlia* (1902) and *On Sunday Morning She Gathered Herbs* (1909), reflect her turn toward depictions of peasant life and the irrational forces of nature.

Kobylians'ka's life revolved around her literary and cultural activity. She never married and had no children. After 1891 she lived in Chernivtsi, a city now in Ukraine. Declining health after 1903, further aggravated during the First World War, reduced her public activity and her writing. She died in Chernivtsi in 1942.

Maxim Tarnawsky
Toronto

TRANSLATIONS OF OL'HA KOBYLIANS'KA'S WORKS

But ... The Lord Is Silent: Selected Prose Fiction by Olha Kobylianska and Yevhenia Yaroshynska. Trans. Roma Franko. Ed. Sonia Morris. Women's Voices in Ukrainian Literature, Volume III. Saskatoon, Saskatchewan: Language Lanterns Publications, 1999.

"Impromptu phantasie." *Written in the Book of Life: Works by 19th-20th Century Ukrainian Writers.* Trans. Mary Skrypnyk. Moscow: Progress, 1982. 140–45.

"Nature." Trans. Percival Cundy. *Their Land: An Anthology of Ukrainian Short Stories.* Ed. Michael Luchkovich. Jersey City, New Jersey: Svoboda Press, 1964. 43–63.

"Sadly the Pine Trees Sway" Trans. by Mary Skrypnyk. *Ukrainian Canadian.* 36. 671 (165) (November 1983): 36–39.

"Time." Trans. by Irene Tavina. *Ukraine.* 11 (87) (November 1983): 22–23.

ABOUT OL'HA KOBYLIANS'KA AND HER WORKS

Solomea Pavlychko. "Modernism vs. Populism in Fin de Siècle Ukrainian Literature: A Case of Gender Conflict." *Engendering Slavic Literatures.* Ed. Pamela Chester and Sibelan Forrester. Bloomington, Indiana: Indiana University Press, 1996. 83–103.

Don't go, Hryts, to the evening revels,
There are enchantresses there.
They burn straw and they cook herbs,
And they will, Hryts, destroy your health.

There is one dark-haired maid,
A true and just enchantress,
An enchantress who knows herbs,
Who loves you most jealously.

On Sunday morning she gathered herbs,
On Monday she soaked them,
On Tuesday she cooked them,
On Wednesday morning she poisoned Hryts.

Thursday came and dear Hryts died
On Friday he was buried.
He was buried near the border,
All the maids cried for him.

And all the boys lamented him,
Everyone cursed the dark-haired maid:
Hryts is no more, there will never be another
Because he has been killed by the enchantress.

On Saturday morning her mother beat her:
"Why, you bitch, did you poison Hryts?
Didn't you know the power of the herbs?
That Hryts will die before the rooster crows?"

"Mother, Mother! Grief has no measure.
Hryts should not love two at a time!
And here is your payment for that, Hryts:
A dark house made of four planks."

On Sunday Morning She Gathered Herbs

It happened long ago. So long ago that no one can say exactly where the events chronicled here took place. Except, perhaps, that it was in the mountains.

Nestled between these mountains rising in a dignified manner on all sides, as though inside a cauldron, hid a fairly large village.

The forests in these mountains were old and impenetrable. At the foot of one of these mountains, named Chabanytsia, against which our village huddled, ran a noisy stream. Frothing and swift, it foamed over huge unmoving boulders, encircling Chabanytsia as if wanting to embrace it. Row upon row, a thick growth of firs, one after another, marched down to the river from the heights, stopping at the bottom right at the river's edge.

They stood there murmuring with green wings outspread, their needles turned upward.... Not like the wild river below them with its loud splashing, roaring and churning, but in their own more discreet and secretive way.

Quietly, mournfully, agitatedly, and on soaring wings, something in the atmosphere lulled into sleep, at the same time giving way to sorrow. Steadily and guardedly, now quietly, now whispering, there was a constant murmur, always with one voice....

The trees grew mournfully on the mountain heights.

Wherever one looked it was one and the same. A sea of verdure in constant, rippling motion.

On the opposite mountain the firs marched with determination in thick rows from the bottom up.

On another they came running down in a mighty arc, their arms extended.

And it was thus everywhere.

Be it summer or winter, good weather or bad, it was always unchanging—always the same song, the same rhythm, the same flow, the same murmur and roar.

* * *

Not far from the river, its garden adjoining Chabanytsia Mountain, lay the grounds of the house and mill of the wealthy widow, Ivanykha Dub, who was known far and wide.

The water foamed, the mill hummed, the firs murmured, and always as one, whether by day or by night, they kept to one rhythm.

The firs grew green, protecting and surrounding with their thick shade the house of this renowned widow, their devout and austere mistress.

Her garden began to flaunt its flowers from the very first days of her marriage.

Beloved by her from early girlhood, they rioted there into deep autumn. And when she was widowed and left with an only child, she had become so accustomed to them that the garden beside her house, though not large, would have seemed to her worse than a desert without them.

The proudest among them were the large red perennial poppies, grown in the village by no one but her.

death

* * *

One day, much to the wonder of its inhabitants, gypsies came to this village locked in the mountains. Not individually, as perhaps one might think, but an entire camp arrived in several wagons. On their way back to Hungary after travelling through many towns and villages, they settled in their tents for a few days right here beside Chabanytsia, a little distance from the village.

The inhabitants, though not timid by nature, became considerably alarmed about this influx of uninvited, dark-skinned guests. Since earliest times, tales about the gypsies had not given rise to a friendly attitude toward them. One legend about the gypsies accused their ancestors of having refused Mary, the baby Jesus, and Joseph refuge for the night, and though not known by everyone, it aroused enmity toward the gypsies. But everyone knew that the gypsies had secret hideouts in various places in the mountains, out of which they emerged to attack travellers—robbing, killing, and enriching themselves with their stolen booty. Then, just as quickly and mysteriously as they appeared, they would disappear, where and how, no one knew. Upon their arrival, the gypsies always built big bonfires at night to announce their presence to the local inhabitants. During the day solitary gypsies wandered

Gypsies (seen in negative light

through the neighboring villages, begging for alms, mending pots, gathering medicinal herbs in the mountains, telling fortunes, playing their violins and dulcimers for a piece of bread or some old clothing, and sometimes, as mentioned before, attacking travellers—and all hurriedly, as though in transitory flight.

Appearing this time at the village below Chabanytsia, they begged permission to remain for about one week. This the inhabitants refused, curtailing their stay by half. In those few days an event occurred among them that was not soon forgotten. Five house-wagons arrived, each covered in dusty tatters out of which peered the frighteningly black, shaggy heads of old and young gypsy women and their children.

Alongside and behind the horse- and donkey-pulled wagons walked the gypsy men, looking about curiously with their shining black eyes.

As mentioned, they pitched their tents not far from the village and the river near Chabanytsia, and immediately, on the first evening, built a large bonfire.

On the third day after their arrival an uproar lasting two days occurred in one of the tents. Exactly three nights after their arrival, young Mavra, the wife of Radu, the chief of the gypsies, gave birth to a son. The father, seeing that the child was amazingly white of skin, assailed the unfortunate mother with threats, curses and beatings, accusing her of betrayal. Mavra's old mother, who, by virtue of her age, was accorded the highest respect in keeping with gypsy custom, defended her with wild cries and imprecations, throwing herself like a whirlwind between her daughter and Radu.

In the meantime, practically all of the men supported the betrayed chief of their tribe: had she not brought dishonour on the entire community of pure-blooded gypsies with her first son? May she not live to see another sunrise, they clamoured and cursed along with the enraged father and chief, who was boiling from the insult and thirsted for revenge, threatening his wife with the whip. Gathered beside the tent of the sinner the men repeated, as though with one voice, the words of their chief: "Already with the first son!..."

"Where did you get this white whelp?" barked Radu from time to time at his sick wife who was lying, barely conscious, among pillows and tatters, hugging and trying to protect the child from the wild, flashing and furious glare of her husband, almost fainting with the terror of what could happen at any moment.

She preferred to die than live through this. She would rather die, but what then? Stupefied with fear, she could not open her mouth to utter a single word....

Radu, who was much older than his wife, stood among the men, dressed in a ceremonial blue waistcoat with large silver buttons and rattles, holding a heavy silvered cane in his hand, a sign that he was the head of this small community. He continued to repeat the same thing over and over:

"Where did you get him? I'll teach you who Radu is. I'll show you whose wife you are!" And he would yank the poor woman's hair so that she groaned in pain. "Just you wait, I'll show you. Before three days are up your bones will not be found in this tent, and as for this accursed child (pointing to the baby), I'll throw him as far as the third mountain. You thought you could marry me and bring shame upon me and the community? Die, bitch, since you did not realize your fortune, or how the wife of a chieftain should conduct herself. Just look!" he threatened, turning to the men, "Look at the son she has brought me after three years of marriage!" He burst into laughter, then hissed through his teeth: "You're lucky that you are still lying here among us, that your father is Andronati and your mother the oldest member of our community. Even so—I will not tolerate your presence here for even these three days," he stamped his foot angrily, spat scornfully once again, and strode out of the tent....

Mavra raked her thin, dark fingers through the dark hair hanging over her low forehead and gave it a weak tug. A deep moan of pain and grief emerged from her young breast ... then falling silent, painfully she closed her tear–filled eyes. The large silver coins plaited into her hair slid low over her brow and gave her dark, bronzed face an enchanting beauty.

* * *

The summer night was bright and peaceful and the dark forested mountains rose like giants into the heavens, the tallest peaks seeming to melt away in the moonlight and the transparent night mist....

Radu stood tall among his gypsies. Only the men were present, lying and sitting around a large bonfire, smoking and discussing what had happened. Some distance away the women and girls busied themselves around another, smaller fire, preparing a meal and looking after the children, feeding them before their bedtime, and discussing with no less passion the fate awaiting the young and beautiful Mavra. They had long envied her the silver and gold necklaces that Radu had given her when he chose her as his wife, and for the fact that she alone earned the most money with her fortune-telling, be it for ordinary people or for the gentry. Now, after three years of marriage she had borne her husband a *white child with blue eyes*!... For shame!

As mentioned, Radu stood among his people and without a word threw his broadbrimmed hat to the ground.

"Radu," spoke up old Andronati, the father of the young, twenty-year-old offender. "Radu, what are you going to do? I know that Mavra is guilty of betrayal and that she must be punished, as is our custom. If we do not punish her ourselves, then her sin may punish her no less harshly. Whether it punishes her now or twenty years hence, she will be punished. What do you want to do? Mavra is guilty," and with these words he bowed submissively before the younger man.

Radu did not reply. Instead, he tore his blue waistcoat open and removed a small bag hanging around his neck.

"Make room!" he roared, "and pay attention!..."

The gypsies stirred silently, making room for their young leader, placing themselves around him curiously and obediently. Meanwhile, like the very tsar of the night, Radu angrily and proudly shook his head with its long black curly hair, the sign of a free spirit. Next he reached into the bag, drew out a handful of shiny gold coins and, as he had done earlier with his hat, threw them to the ground and shouted:

"This, the first time, to the one...."

Then repeating what he had done, he shouted again:

"This, the second time, to the one.... And this, the third time, to the one who will remove the woman who has betrayed me from my sight within two days, and her white whelp with her!..."

There was instant silence among the gypsies, but not for long. They stirred, first like the strumming of bass guitar strings, then like the rustle of leaves....

They all knew that the traditional punishment for betrayal was severe, but what had transpired this night had never before happened among them. How many fights and acts of violence had occurred among them! But no matter how many such incidents had taken place, it had never before come to pass that their leader himself stood before them and commanded that his wife be banished, paying for it with pure gold. Only an implacable mind, maddened by jealousy, like Radu's could have concocted something like this.

In that first moment they were speechless, not knowing what to say or how to react. This brutal decision of their chieftain had caught them too unexpectedly.

But the silence among the frightened gypsies did not continue for long. Mavra's old father, Andronati, a tall, thin, bearded gypsy, rose again to his feet. He was the finest musician among them, and even now, as he stood there, he was holding his violin.

"Wait, Radu," he said, snaking his hand into the air, "wait, Radu. There is a God above all of us. We are all his children, the whites, the gypsies, Radu, and Mavra. You cannot decide...."

Radu opened his mouth to utter a savage imprecation, interrupting the old man, but Andronati continued:

"You, Radu, were the only son of your father, a chieftain in Transylvania, and Mavra is the only child of Andronati, the famous musician from the Hungarian plain. And you married. Therefore you are the same to me as Mavra, and Mavra the same as you. I will not allow you to remove Mavra or put her to death as you so obviously wish, though I know that our custom decrees that all betrayal, be it by man or woman, must be punished severely. Neither would I permit your own destruction if someone or other should suggest it in similar circumstances. We will judge Mavra in another way, charitably and humanely. Give her another three days among us, her father, Andronati, is asking this of you himself." Having said this, Andronati again bowed to the still youthful chieftain.

"She is a choice adultress. Pray God that she not live to see the sunrise!" once again shouted the agitated and infuriated husband.

"Maybe she will not see the morning," answered Andronati. "You have become exceedingly eager for her life. She may leave us forever by herself and your gold ducats will then remain with you."

"Let her go, let her go!" the voices of the gathered gypsies rose. "She has brought us shame with her first son, her first child. What next? Out with her, she herself has chosen her path," shouted a voice from the group, "out with her!"

"No, she must be killed so that she will not do this to another man!" hissed Radu. "Killed!"

"In three days Mavra will no longer be among you," Andronati spoke up again. "Her fate has already been decided by the baby that you would tear to pieces if Mavra were to remain among us. Everyone would mistreat the child. This way ... she will leave us and be out of Radu's sight."

"You will kill her yourself?" asked a voice out of the group, the voice of Andronati's friend—the dulcimer player.

"Myself."

"Then take the gold coins."

"No, I leave them for you. Feed yourselves with them. You are all younger than I am. I do not need them. From today on Mavra has ceased to be mine. I do not need them. I can still find bread for myself and my wife." And with a proud gesture he thrust his violin before him, threatening the young chieftain with his fist.

"What about your daughter's whelp?" asked Radu haughtily, flashing a malevolent glance at his unflinching father-in-law. "I don't need him. I'll kill him, crush him like a serpent!"

"Don't worry about him. I will take responsibility for him. It ...," and suddenly he stopped. Mavra's old mother had emerged from one of the tents like a phantom, haggard, dishevelled, a silver necklace gleaming under the moon's rays lying on her chest. Rushing out, she immediately threw herself at the feet of Radu and Andronati.

"Forgive Mavra, if she has sinned," she wailed, holding out her arms beseechingly, "don't destroy a young woman! Beat her, strike her, but let her live! Oh, Mavra, Mavra, what have you done? What got into you? What evil wind has blown your way? From which direction? From the valleys or the mountains? Mavra, my daughter ... my heart ... Mavra!" she lamented in an inhuman voice. "I bathed you in herbs in the light of the moon and there wasn't a night when I did not pray for your good fortune. When you were but a tiny babe, I fed you honey, sheltered you from evil eyes until you married.... I protected you as though from fire. Then evil times came and with them your enemy ... and now look.... Help her, have pity.... Give her to me at least for a few days, at least until we reach the Hungarian plain.... Let me bring her there, then kill her if you will, and me, as well," and she hurled herself forward, her head hitting the ground.

"Out of the way, old woman!" cried Andronati. "Why have you come crawling? To be beaten? Have you already forgotten? Don't rely too much on your hoary head. Away, I tell you, out of here, can't you see that we men are in council, passing judgement? Here he turned toward Radu: "Give me your final word after I say mine. Permit Mavra to stay with us at least for four days to recover her strength, so that her father can play for her among you for the last time. To bid her farewell among you. Then either forgive her or do what you will, chieftain," he bowed again humbly, as before.

"I will not forgive Mavra. I do not want to set eyes on her again. She will not live among us!" Radu responded stubbornly. "She has only herself to blame."

"Herself ... herself...," echoed the crowd in an ingratiating murmur, "only herself."

"This is your final word, Radu?" asked Andronati, while the mother began to wail anew, burrowing her fingers in her grey hair.

"Final."

Saying this, again he began to repeat what he had said earlier, throwing handfuls of gold coins on the ground.

"This, the first time, to the one...."

"This, the second time, to the one...."

"This, the third time, to the one who will free me in any way from the cursed betrayer in four days. Have you heard my word?"

"We have."

Upon hearing these words, Andronati the musician rose to his feet. He stood up and looked about him with a strange expression in his eyes. A terrible fire blazed in those shining black eyes. He shoved his violin under his arm and said:

"I am going. I shall return in the evening of the day after tomorrow. We will be together again. Good health to you."

Bending over his wife, who lay on the ground as though she were taking leave of her senses, he shouted:

"Why are you going mad? Go to Mavra. No one will dare touch her now. After tomorrow she will no longer be with us, but you will answer to me for her safety while I am gone. I am leaving now, but I shall return the day after tomorrow. Everyone will gather here in the evening, like today. In the meantime, consult with each other as to who among you will take the gold pieces our chieftain is offering for Mavra. I am going...."

And he left.

* * *

On the third evening he returned.

The gypsies were already waiting in a circle in various poses, Radu among them, pale and restless as a demon. Just a few moments before he had fought with the mother of his sick wife, who had pushed him out of Mavra's tent.

It was unheard of in the gypsy clans for a woman to lift a hand against a man, as Mavra's mother had done in defence of that traitress. But he would teach them all. All of them. The old and the young. To defend a traitress? He would teach her, the old woman and....

Here Andronati appeared among them as they sat, with his violin under his arm.

He gave the violin to his friend, the dulcimer player, who had come with him, then pulled out a large, flask-like bottle of whiskey and set it down in the centre of the circle.

"Drink heartily, brothers," he called out, "drink, and don't begrudge yourselves. Andronati is bidding farewell to his Mavra today, so remember this night! Mavra!" he cried out, pounding his chest with his fist,—"Mavra!"—his voice trembling with sudden emotion, "You cannot come among us any more, my little cuckoo.... But you are not alone there. Your mother is beside you, and all your wives, my brothers—so that she will not guess that tomorrow is her last day among us. But little cuckoo," and he turned toward her tent, "Andronati is bidding farewell to you before his brothers and your husband—our chieftain—saying goodbye so that they will remember." Here his voice trembled and gave way. "Throw some more fir branches on the fire," he cried, as though giving assurance to his voice with those words, "so that it will flame and light up the whole mountain; so that it will blaze up and announce that Mavra is saying goodbye to the gypsies. Drink up and don't begrudge yourselves. Blow on the coals, stoke the flames, so that starting from today they will warm Mavra's soul when she is far away. Drink, brothers, drink! Andronati, the musician, entreats you. Drink, don't begrudge yourselves. Who knows where we shall all end up and how soon ... or if Andronati will remain here among you. Mavra will be no more among us.... And there will be no more poor Andronati.... Enough.... As fate has decreed for each one. Her destiny was being nicely arranged.... Drink!"

And Andronati walks about, generously pouring out drinks for everyone, but seeming to forget to refill his own, all the while wiping tears from his eyes.

Radu lay on the ground resting his head on one elbow and not saying a word, as if he were there all by himself.

He drank one whiskey after another, poured by Andronati into a small silver goblet that had been passed down in the family as a highly treasured object, his thoughts constantly on Mavra. He was almost beside himself with rage. What good was she to him now? She has a lying heart. When he took her she assured him that she loved him and then she betrayed him ... and with someone outside their own clan, to boot. He was beginning to guess with whom. In a small town near the Hungarian plain where they sometimes settled and where her father often earned money playing his violin, while she told fortunes, sang to his accompaniment, and sometimes even danced, there was a young boyar. He always offered a great deal of money for gypsy music and sometimes, with his friends, would gallop past their tents like a whirlwind into the Hungarian plain. With him. But she no longer matters to him. Never mind that she is beautiful, never mind that even though she is young, she is the best fortune-teller among them, or that she is the daughter of Andronati the musician, renowned among the gypsies—she is no longer his wife. He has thrown his gold ducats among his people, let them do with her what they will. Kill her, or throw her out somewhere. It makes no difference to him. He cares only that he be revenged, that she be taken out of his sight, dead or alive. Otherwise it will come to no good between them. And because of her he will not leave his clan, just so as not to see her. That means that *she* must get out of his sight. But how? It does not matter.... He is totally indifferent to her now. Unless, of course, if he would beat her. Otherwise, he is indifferent to her.

Indifferent? At this thought his despondent glance suddenly crept like a thief toward the tent where the guilty woman lay, and gazed penetratingly at it.

Indifferent?

Damned woman! She betrayed *him*—betrayed the first chieftain among the gypsy clans.

All around him people were drinking and murmuring about him and Mavra, either united in their opinions or arguing about them. Here and there the women made their voices heard. He had to stay there and drink with them, though his soul burned with bitterness, like the blaze which was leaping and crackling from the dry, red fir branches fed into the bonfire. That is how it was burning in his soul. But he had to remain through it all. He had to do everything for the last time, for himself, for the people, and for Andronati whom the people greatly respected.

Suddenly there was a movement.

Andronati was making the rounds for the last time, generously offering whiskey, not sparing a drop, filling almost everyone's glass to overflowing. Then he picks up his violin and stands before them.

"My people!" he shouted, "take up the dulcimer, the flutes, and those who are with me, your violins. Mavra!" he turned to the tent housing his daughter, "Mavra! Say goodbye to Radu. At this time tomorrow you will not be ours any more," and he pulled the bow. Bending his head low over his violin and as if hearing within it a secret, private voice for himself alone, he began to play.

*   *   *

The music poured forth sorrow.

The violins wept, the dulcimer tinkled, the flutes trembled, but above them all one string from Andronati's violin held sway. Ah, that violin! It wailed, its voice wandered, overflowing with sadness, it surged among the gypsies, recounting the story of Mavra and Radu.

And once again, sorrow....

Like a delicate bee it sang plaintively, fluttered, then flowed headlong, evoking melancholy and sadness, dissolving into grief.

Andronati was playing a doina.[3]

"Mavra," he cried out despairingly from time to time, oblivious of his savage sorrow, and keeping time with his foot. "Mavra!" He played, his whole body swaying like a madman. "Mavra! It is your father playing.... *sad or* Andronati is playing for you among the gypsies for the last time. Perhaps, *hear?* after this, you will hear him no more. Mavra!"

Radu lay there with his face turned to the ground, giving himself up to only one emotion. She had betrayed him. Betrayed him and he will never touch her again. Unless in anger. He will kill her! He cannot do otherwise, it is not in his nature. He cannot ... he cannot. It seemed as though the voice of the violin had attached itself only to his shattered soul, thirsty for revenge, and like a wasp, kept digging in and irritating it. "She has brought me a white child from another man, a stranger." The violin shuddered and wept, the dulcimer sorrowed. "Some stranger...." With these feelings of grief and jealousy his thoughts passed into delirium. "A white child ... in the third year of our marriage.... Mav-ra! Damn you for your betrayal. May all misfortune be on your head!"

The moon stood burning full from behind the tall, forested mountain.

"Radu!" Mavra's voice suddenly seemed to reach out to him, and Andronati's violin fell, shattering beside Radu's head. "Radu!" He shuddered as Andronati also fell to the ground next to him.

"Mav-ra, Mav-ra! We are saying goodbye to you forever.... For-e-ver," the old man groaned, then after a long moment of silence, he begged: "Sleep, my people, sleep. Spend this one last night beside her and tomorrow, those of you who desire it, can bring an end to her. Those who took the gold pieces offered by Radu, let them also take her soul. Is that not so, Radu?"

"It is so," the chieftain's voice responded curtly.

"Then back to the Hungarian plain—the broad limitless plain. U-kha, the plain! U-kha!" the musician cried out wildly, "but today you can still sleep. And old Andronati with all of you." He sat up, folding his legs beneath him and burying his fingers in his hair, sobbing bitterly. He had to part with his

---

3. A very moving type of Romanian gypsy music.

Mavra, there was no way out. The punishment for betrayal, especially for women and particularly for wives of chieftains, had to be carried out. He understood the gravity of her transgression better than most—and this was her last night among them—her gypsy clan.

"Sleep, people," he entreated, "sleep, Radu. Look! Everything has been decided. If this is her punishment, then let it be so. The moon is witness to it all, our brother moon who never abandons us. Sleep, people. Sleep, Mavra. Sleep, Radu, young and orphaned chieftain. You are my children. Hush, everyone, let her have a good rest on this last night among us. Sleep, everyone. Sleep, Mavra. Sleep, Radu ... only the Hungarian plain awaits us now ... the broad, still plain. Hush ... sleep.... Mavra is sleeping.... Hush ... sleep...."

Silence fell. The camp slept.

*   *   *

It was close to one o'clock that same night that Mavra, the beautiful young wife of the gypsy chieftain, and her white son departed forever from him, from his tent and his life.

The gypsies, together with Radu, slept like the dead. Only two among them slid out from their midst with cat-like movements—old Andronati and his loyal fellow musician. They had both agreed earlier not to drink as much as the rest so that while the camp slept they could carry Mavra and her child out, steal her away from Radu and death, or, at the very least, from some kind of mutilation. The decrees issued by gypsy chieftains were often terrible. So after discussing and letting no one else in on their secret, they decided to remove Mavra from the camp earlier than the agreed-upon four days. They believed that once she was removed from the camp she would be safe. Mavra was intelligent and clever and more than likely would build herself a new life before they ever met again. Andronati would lay the child at the door of some wealthy childless couple—maybe in one of the villages beyond Chabanytsia Mountain, and all would be well. Better this way than to die or be crippled for the rest of her life. Radu often liked to avenge himself by crippling his enemies and this is what her father feared could happen to Mavra.

When everyone had fallen sound asleep from the sleeping potion that Andronati had put in their drink, herbs for which he had spent two days hunting in the mountains, Andronati and his friend carried Mavra and her child out of the camp.

She would not die like some animal, his young and beautiful only child, she would live. Live among good people and far away. The world is big, God feeds all his children, and He will feed her as well. She can hardly remain with Radu. Radu will revenge himself on her throughout her entire life, beginning as soon as she is able to stand on her feet. In spite of his good looks and wisdom beyond his years, in his malice and vindictiveness he took after his famous father, the former chieftain of the Transylvanian gypsy clan.

* * *

Mavra, who had also been made to drink the sleeping potion, slept like the dead and sensed nothing when they carried her out, with only the moon and the stars as witness.

Andronati's teeth chattered, his body sagged with grief as they carried out their plan. But better to leave her to the kindness of strangers than see her killed or maimed for life. He might still be able to see her sometime in the future, find her sooner or later during his lifetime, but to live and see her crippled would be worse than death.

They walked beside the noisy river that churned and frothed below the precipice of Chabanytsia Mountain, dashing wildly and impetuously against the huge boulders in its bed.

They headed in the opposite direction from the camp until they found a suitable spot some distance from the village, but still frequented by its inhabitants. They left Mavra under a tall spreading fir not far from the mill of the recently-widowed Ivanykha Dub.

The gypsies considered the fir a holy tree and a good friend—a guardian against death. It now offered the only protection for the unfortunate Mavra until some charitable human soul would have mercy on her. Next to the sleeping woman they placed a bundle of her belongings, and the gold coins that Andronati's good friend had gathered off the ground.

Then they left.

The friend went ahead to lie down again in his place so as not to arouse any suspicions. Andronati went later. He returned for a moment to be alone with his daughter.

She was still sleeping

After sobbing bitter tears at her side and pronouncing some magic words to protect her from harm in the future, he picked up her white-skinned baby son and left. He held him closely, tenderly, at the same time cursing the enemy who had ruined his mother and brought her to this unfortunate end, never to stand before God, but to wander endlessly about the world in wretchedness and grief, hunger and cold. A curse on him.

Where was he taking the orphan? he asked himself. He had no idea. To what father and mother? He does not know them—has not seen or heard of them—but he plods on. Will he leave him somewhere at a fortunate hour? He will curse the enemy as long as there is life in him. And his curses are terrible. Everyone was afraid of them, because they came true.

And he walked on.

He followed a narrow path up the mountainside that began near the widow Dub's mill, circled Chabanytsia on the right, hid itself in the forest, then emerged again over the deep, dark ravine through which a noisy, rushing stream made its way. This White Path, as it was called by the local inhabitants, climbed up the hill, then descended, following the ups and downs of the mountainside on the right side of the ravine that separated Chabanytsia from the neighbouring rocky mountain, which faced Chabanytsia with its precipitous, tree-covered cliffside. The White Path trailed through Chabanytsia's thick forest, meandered through the lovely mountain meadows and small tilled fields, remaining narrow and white to its very end, where it seemed to dissolve into an intersecting road that swallowed and cut it off from further travel.

In the greyness of early morning Andronati entered the third village from Chabanytsia, a village that lay closer to another mountain rising right at the Hungarian border. Although he had not been walking long, he was perspiring heavily. He sat down to rest at the forest's edge and looked about. The sun was just rising in the east and the firs breathed the cold fragrance of resin. The dawn was advancing toward daylight but the holy quiet of early morning continued to reign.

Slumber still held sway.

Resting there with his white grandson in his arms, Mavra's old father, his soul quaking with anxiety, searched the village below with sharp eyes. He could not find what he sought.

There in the valley, in the village below Chabanytsia Mountain, in the forest near the rapid-flowing river, where only the solitary mill and the river sounded, he had abandoned his sick daughter like an animal, so that her own people would not maim or destroy her. And here he is holding her unfortunate son in order to lay him at the door of a couple of wealthy, childless strangers down below, and somehow he has no luck.

A grey mist clouding the village refuses to rise, as if purposely refusing to reveal a path for him to walk on, to point out the home of a wealthy landowner. But the day is becoming brighter and time is passing.

He sighed deeply. What had his life come to? What was he to do now? Yesterday he broke his violin in sorrow while playing a farewell song for his daughter, left his wife behind and went off. Would he find her alive when he returned? He knew gypsies as only a gypsy can know them, knew what seethed within them, what happens among them, what gypsy life is like. Here today, there tomorrow—and the day after tomorrow, perhaps even dead. Suddenly he recalled a tale, an almost thousand-year-old legend, about the reasons behind the gypsies' eternal wanderings and their hardships. While still in Egypt, they had refused to allow Mary and Joseph with the holy child to rest among them. From time immemorial they had to wander throughout the world in punishment. Would it ever end, this divine retribution? Would they ever atone for their sin?

He smiled bitterly, as though in his sleep.

The punishment would probably continue as long as the gypsy race existed.

The step he had taken with his daughter and her innocent white child, was it not another punishment, another form of penance? Dear God, have pity on your sinful people—they repent. In destitution and humility, in hunger and in cold, they painfully repent.

Whispering these words, he waits.

The mist continues to hang over the village. Is it deliberately barring the child's entry? Could this be his legacy? Is he also to await an obscure fate in the future?

The sun is on the verge of rising, its rosy rays are just about to appear, but the mist stubbornly remains.

But what is this?

The voice of a trembita sounds from the opposite mountain, separated from him by a small valley.

So early in the morning?

Yes, it really is the voice of the mountain horn announcing something sadly, in a drawn-out manner, like a distinct sorrow. It seems to Andronati that its voice is unloading all its grief onto him. The silence around him is profound—not a branch sways, but simultaneously the voice of the trembita moves along the heights. Just like Andronati.

Unable to control himself, Andronati sobbed at the sound. The wail of the trembita bode nothing good so early in the morning. He looked up at the sun. Flaming blood-red, exquisite and blinding, it appeared over the mountain summit. The mist in the valley finally grew lighter. He got up then, moved down the path into the valley and then up again. There on the rise stood a splendid homestead, its appearance proclaiming affluence. Around it, just like in the forest, everything slumbered. With silent steps he walked up to the banked earth around the house and carefully placed his sleeping grandson upon it.

He looked about.

Has he placed the boy there at an auspicious moment? There's no telling. God grant that it be a good one.

Would the fate of the child be revealed?

There was no answer to his thoughts. Silence reigned—there was not a rustle, not a movement, not a sound to be heard. As the saying goes, sleep itself was still breathing. But the morning mists continued to flow delicately upward, concealing everything from his sight.

* * *

When he returned to the path he met a shepherd whom he stopped immediately, and asked:

"Why was the trembita sounding before sunrise, and not only sounding, but sobbing?"

"Some wealthy man must have died. A poor peasant has no sheep or meadow, so the trembita would not sorrow for him," answered the shepherd shortly and began to descend the hill as though on wings.

"Whoa!" Andronati called out after him when he had gone some distance.

The shepherd stopped reluctantly.

"What is it?"

"Whose homestead it that up there on the rise, with the haystacks near the house?" he asked, pointing to the farmhouse where he had left his grandchild.

"It belongs to the richest man in the village. You don't know him?"

"No, I'm a stranger."

"It belongs to Mykhailo Donchuk," the shepherd added.

"Does he have children?"

"Not a single one. Instead he has hundreds of sheep and a herd of horses. There...." And, in his hurry, without finishing his sentence, the shepherd waved a hand to indicate that the man was very well off, then he vanished among the trees.

Andronati, too, walked on without looking back again, wiping the tears that were forcing themselves out of his eyes.

He walked in a sea of resinous fragrance wafting in the clean morning air. The firs seemed to have lost themselves within it and dreaming, forgot all movement.

High up in the heavens two birds of prey flew in easy flowing circles, gazing down in search of spoils for the day.

Finding himself on the crest of the mountain from which the Hungarian border could be seen, Andronati suddenly recalled his abandoned gypsy camp.

What was happening there?

Nothing good, he was sure. He could imagine Radu's rage.

The situation must certainly have ended in a fight, or even murder. Maybe his wife will suffer for all of them?

Probably not. They are all afraid of her. She is terrifying and mighty in the strength of her sorcery. What is more, she is the eldest of the women in the community and because of the respect given by the gypsies to the oldest woman, she is protected against all attacks. Radu, though vengeful and quick to react, will not dare cause her any harm. But perhaps his friend had suffered after returning to the sleepers in the tent and awakening him. Radu did not completely trust him, accusing him of considering Andronati, a poor musician, the chieftain and not Radu. Whatever happened, it was a good thing that Mavra had been snatched from his hands. Whatever fate awaited her now among strangers, especially in the beginning, at least she will remain alive, will not be a cripple. Her child, too, though his father is not a gypsy, will live, and not be killed like an animal. Good people will take pity on them and take them in. Neither the mother nor the son will suffer among them. In time, perhaps, if he is still among the living, he will find them and they will join another gypsy community. By that time Radu's anger will also have cooled.

Poor Mavra. What will your awakening be like in the forest beneath the fir?

Mavra! His soul cried out in pain, his father's heart wept and again the tears overflowed his eyes. He walked on blindly, almost feeling his way by touch. Never before in his life had he experienced such bitter pain as during these past few days. Better that she had died in childhood than be orphaned and wasted in the best years of her life. For what? He clasped his hands together in despair.

When had sin enticed her into its web?

She had no right so much as to touch a strange man, yet she had sinned.... God Almighty! He had already guessed when it may have happened—when she began to go out among the gentry to read fortunes and sing sad songs to the accompaniment of his violin, in order to satisfy Radu's insatiable greed with the gold pieces she brought back as payment. It was then that the wolf had appeared and become enamoured with her youth and beauty—leading to that. And what about his own wretched self? Where should he turn now? It might be best if he goes directly to the Hungarian plain and joins another clan, then summons his wife. Yes, there is no other way. And some day, perhaps in a few years—he will wander back to these parts and see how his grandchild is thriving in that wealthy household. In a few years.... In the meantime, pray the Lord keep his eye on him. On him and Mavra.

Amen

* * *

For a long, long time the musician gazed fixedly at the tops of the forested mountains that seemed to be shedding their early morning fog, jutting out one ridge after another against the sun that, having risen in the east, was glowing with light, blinding to the eyes.

* * *

Mavra awoke early. She realized that she was in a forest when she saw the green branches of a fir tree instead of a dust-covered and tattered tent roof above her. At first, she did not know what to think upon finding herself alone, without her people, without Radu, her mother or father, who had never left her before now.

She began calling out, but her voice echoed weakly through the forest and summoned no one.

She lay there for some time, waiting for her mother, and listening.

Her mother did not come.

No one came.

She was surrounded by silence. Only the broad, winged murmur of the forest, swaying with resinous fragrance, and the rustle of a squirrel scampering like lightning through the branches some place or other could be heard. Here and there, the sun's gold rays peeped between the fir branches—and somewhere, not too far away, the roar of a river sounded, along with the din of a mill.

So she was somewhere near a mill.

But why was she by herself? Where was her mother? Where were the tents, the camp? Why was there none of the bustle of people around her, the voice of her father, no curses or commands from Radu or the ringing sounds of copper kettles being repaired? Nothing. Why was it like this? Only silence and more silence, and she, lying here all alone?

What has happened?

Has she been abandoned? Oh, God!

How could this have happened? Abandoned by her mother?

"Mother, mother!" she began to call in feverish terror, her hair standing on end. Has she really been abandoned? "Mother!" she called with growing fear and began to cry. She sobbed unrestrainedly, like a little child, calling her mother and then her father, by turns. When neither appeared she stopped, as though eyes had opened up in her soul. This was Radu's work. He had thrown her out of his tent and driven her away. He had taken everyone, her father and mother, his people, and like the wind run away in the night, as was his custom. This was Radu's work. He promised he would have revenge for her betrayal, for the white child, and he did as he promised. "Oh-h-h!" she wept loudly, swaying back and forth, digging her fingers into her hair in despair.

She stopped suddenly.

In a flash she remembered her baby and was silenced.

She forced herself to her feet and began to search all around. There was no child. There was a bundle of all her things, even the smallest trifle, but there was no child. Half-fainting from shock, she sank back to the ground. Now she understood. It was as she had first guessed—Radu had thrown her out and taking everyone, the baby and her parents, had left secretly during the night.

She began to call out, scream. She called everyone she knew by name, among them her father and mother, even Radu himself, to no avail. No one appeared.

Around her everything was the same: the rustle of the pines, the silence, the solitude—and nothing else. No one and nothing.

Large beads of sweat dotted her forehead. Her mind was transfixed by one terrible thought. Her father, mother, Radu, and the entire clan had abandoned her because of her betrayal, her white child. Abandoned. They had thrown her out like the rags that covered her body, and left. Again she began sobbing loudly. She now understood everything and gave herself up to the depths of despair. But moments later she recovered her reason. Her baby!... Lord God, Merciful and Good, where was her baby? Did they take it? Steal it? Kill it? What had they done with her child, her precious child?

Again she burst into tears, her heart rent with pain.

What will happen now? Where is her child? And for the hundredth time she picks through the bundles left beside her, searching for the child. It is not there. She cannot find it anywhere. Tears will not help her now, nor lamentation—nothing will help now. She will have to search in a different way.

"It was you, Radu, who did this!" she cries aloud, raising her slender arms in desperation. "It was you. You promised to kill it, like a dog—and you did. But then why not kill Mavra as well as the child? But you...." She breaks off suddenly and falls into despair, pulls at her hair, beats her chest, tears at her clothes ... pauses to listen, then sinks anew into despair—all for nothing.

There is no child.

She is surrounded only by her scattered, torn clothing, the thick forest, and the rustle of trees.

Weakened by her tears and despair, she lay down and was silent. Hot tears from beneath her closed lids continued to slide down her pale, emaciated face.

All was lost. He had promised revenge and carried it out. He killed the baby, abandoned her, and she must die. She does not have the strength to follow them, so she must lie here and die, or wait until someone comes through the forest, maybe some of her own people. Maybe they were forced to leave the village, and had only left her here temporarily, and would come later and take her away.

Perhaps.... But the child? The child belongs to her.

She lies there listening....

All around it is completely quiet, except for the rustle of the forest. Somewhere nearby a mill wheel rumbles ... a river roars ... but God only knows where they are.... God only knows where there are any people.

She begins to cry again, call out. Attempting to rise, she realizes that she is still very weak, can barely stand. Dear God, what is she to do?

She sinks back to the ground face down, her body shaking in a frenzy of weeping and despair. She hears nothing, is aware of nothing, only grief and pain. Her body burns with some inner fire.

What does she have left now? She has no child. No child!

Killed!

Her eyes dim, there is a ringing in her ears, a great weakness envelops her ... heat ... darkness.... She is lost.

* * *

Suddenly someone is shaking her, lifting her.

"Are you sleeping, woman? Don't sleep!"

Willing her eyes open, she slowly regains consciousness. The tall figure of an older woman is bent over her, probably some noblewoman, and beside her are some people—men and women.

The woman, or lady, pale and thin, her head wrapped in a black shawl, is looking down at her kindly, saying:

"Get up and come with me—you will stay with me. You are ill. You have been lying here for more than a day. My people will take you slowly to my house."

Mavra, still unable to comprehend what is happening, listens and tries to get up.

Those present, and especially the women, looked with great interest at this unfortunate, abandoned young woman with beautiful, sorrow-filled eyes, dark as night, who lay there like a large wounded bird, surrounded by scattered rags, clothing, and here and there among them, gold coins. Though young and beautiful, she was deathly pale and almost frightening, her dishevelled black hair spread over her back and breasts.

"Where are my people—the gypsies?" she asks weakly in a foreign accent.

"Apparently they have abandoned you," explains the tall, thin woman in black, who had said she would look after her. "They must have abandoned you."

Mavra's eyes grow large, her lips tremble.

"When?" she asks.

"Just recently, I think. People said that they fought among themselves about some theft, a man was wounded—a dulcimer player—and then, dispersing among their wagons, they left during the night. No one even saw them leave. You were found last night by people who came to my mill early this morning, but I couldn't take you into my home until now. Besides, you were in a deep sleep—it was as if you were dead. What happened to you?"

"I don't know," answers Mavra, looking in wonder and almost blindly at the strange people around her, then remembering her baby, bursts into bitter tears again, lifting her arms imploringly and saying something in a language those around her do not understand.

She is interrupted by Ivanykha Dub, for it is none other than this lady, who begins lifting her to her feet with the aid of the others.

"Where did my people go?" asks Mavra.

Nobody knew. To Hungary, it seems.

But what has happened to my child?

They did not know either. *She had a child*?

Yes. A son. *A white son.* Her first child. She is the wife of Radu, the chieftain of the gypsies. Did her people take the child with them? They did not know. They could not guess what they had not seen. Immediately after the fight the gypsies had disappeared in the night.

Then maybe they had killed her child?

No, they didn't know.

They must have killed it!

No, they hadn't heard. They had only heard that one man in the fight had nearly been killed by the gypsy chieftain.

"Oh, Radu," Mavra groaned, wringing her hands and breaking into sobs again, "I'm sure he killed the baby, too."

They didn't know. They did not know and could not imagine how anyone could kill an innocent child.

"Oh, Radu!" Mavra sobbed louder in her agitation, "he is so terribly mean once he becomes angry," then added:

"Could it be they stole the baby from me and then fled?"

Perhaps. They didn't know this either.

Oh, it could only be that, if they have disappeared as though the earth has swallowed them up. They must have stolen him. They always did this.... And after the loss of her child she realizes what Radu is like.

"Perhaps," the people answered.

Did anybody at all see a child?

No one.

It was *white*.

Maybe. They didn't know.

"It was white, *white*!" she almost screamed.

They did not know.

The people stood helplessly silent while her sobs grew louder, as if they were loath to betray some secret. Or maybe they did not want to say anything so as not to wound the unfortunate woman with their information. Or perhaps they truly did not know.

* * *

They led the young, orphaned gypsy step by step into the house of Ivanykha Dub and there she remained.

* * *

Why Radu wanted to kill her, or rather revenge himself on her, Mavra told only Ivanykha Dub, and she, in turn, took her into her home.

Two months after the death of her husband, Ivanykha Dub, though no longer young, had given birth to a child, little Tetiana, and Mavra looks after her. Having become a widow, Ivanykha Dub has so much to oversee on her property and at the mill that her only child, who is the apple of her eye and her greatest happiness, must have someone to look after her. Mavra is still weak, unable to do any heavy work, and without the energy to go looking for her people, why not stay with her as long as she wants, Mistress Dub told her. Since many people come to the mill, she urged, someone among them may have heard something about her baby. She may find out what really happened. Or her own people might return for her and she will hear about it soonest here, at the mill.

Mavra heeded this advice and stayed.

Still, she could not bear the widow's quiet home below Chabanytsia for long. She stayed until her strength returned, but after recovering, threw herself into a search for her child and her clan. She walked and wandered for weeks and months at a time, like a hungry she-wolf, returning thin and pale, with bloodless lips and sullen, sad eyes, to live with Ivanykha Dub once again.

Her people had disappeared, gone underground, as was their habit, and there was no trace of them or her child. Nobody knew anything, they did not know and had not heard.

Mavra stopped crying. She realized that nothing would help. She had cried out all her tears, but her beautiful eyes remained full of sadness, never looking anyone boldly in the face. She was ashamed. To her shame, her husband, parents, and people had cast her out like a dog, to the laughter and derision of strangers.

What could be worse than that?

It seemed she was destined to remain forever with the wealthy Ivanykha Dub and look after her child. And because she needed sustenance for her awakened maternal feelings, she became a second mother to little Tetiana. In time Tetiana became like her own child and she was appeased, almost forgetting her own.

Thus she lived, looking after and expending great efforts over another woman's child, until the longing and habits of her strange people to change her place of residence from time to time awakened within her. Then she was seized with a deep yearning to wander somewhere into the wider world.

She would then bid farewell to the child, weeping bitterly, and bowing low to Ivanykha, her hands crossed humbly over her breasts. Bowing low she would kiss the woman's hands and knees and depart. Ivanykha Dub, who had become accustomed to her presence and grown to love her for the affection and generosity to her daughter, would become angry with her ... though in keeping with her dignified nature, she never voiced this anger. Her eyes and her silence spoke for her and would refuse to release Mavra. As has already been said, she loved the orphaned gypsy woman and was sincerely grateful for the genuine motherly care she gave the child.

"Where will you go, all by yourself, into the far, unknown world?" she reproached her. "Have you gone mad? Are you not angering the Lord by leaving your livelihood so easily, and people and a child who are attached to you: Why are you going, for what reason ... and by which road? Could this be God's punishment on you for a second time?"

"No," answered the gypsy woman sadly. She must go out into the world. Her heart burns with a desire to feel the earth beneath her feet. Her peace of mind has flown somewhere into an unknown distance and is now drawing her along with it. She must change her place, she explains. Perhaps she will meet her father and mother, find them at last, maybe see at least one of her former people, meet with them. Perhaps, after all these years, a happy hour will unite her again with her son, her father and mother, maybe even Radu.... She knows when and what roads the gypsies take from Hungary or Moldavia, and when they return. She knows the signs they leave behind for others on trees, stones, by the roadside and so on.

She has to go, something is giving her no rest. If she does not leave, she will become ill from loneliness and grief.... She feels that it is making her sick, so she must go.... Why should she stay?

She will go!

"She wants to go because of Radu, so that he will beat her properly?" asks Ivanykha Dub dryly, gazing fixedly at Mavra, who listens silently.

"So be it. I'm not afraid. If I do not find or meet anyone, I shall return. I have no one in the world besides you, Mistress" (which is what she called Ivanykha Dub, who was always clad in black).

"And the child, how can you leave her?" asked Ivanykha, pointing to little Tetiana who was prowling between them, listening carefully to both women as though she understood that her nurse was leaving her, perhaps forever.

"Oh!" wailed Mavra, weeping loudly, "do not burden Mavra's poor heart even more!" But once she calmed down, she left.

The village folk, seeing her leave loaded down with sacks filled with herbs and tatters, laughed at her.

"Just look," they jeered, "Mavra is going out into the world again. She is going to look for a young gypsy for herself. One of her is not enough in the village. She is overcome with sadness in the widow's house."

She defended herself by heaping bitter curses on them, her beautiful, oblong, sad eyes flashing sparks of pride in their direction as she left.

After a few months, and sometimes even after a year of wandering, she would suddenly appear again below Chabanytsia, tired and discouraged, but weeping with joy to see how Tetiana had grown in her absence and how overjoyed the girl was that Mavra had returned, more so than if it were her own mother returning. She would fall again at the feet of Ivanykha Dub, as she had when she was leaving, kissing her knees and begging:

"Please take me back again for little Tetiana, illustrious Mistress. I should have listened to you and not my gypsy blood. I have only suffered among strangers, received nothing but chiding, reproaches and jeers. I have come back without having found anyone—neither father or mother, nor did I hear anything about my child or my people, or Radu himself. I got only what I bargained for among strangers with my miracle herbs and my fortune-telling ... and look, I've brought some gifts for you and my little precious one." And before the dignified Ivanykha Dub and her little daughter she laid out some commonplace delicacies which she herself passionately loved to eat.

A few years after her last wanderings, when Tetiana's twelfth birthday was nearing, Mavra approached Ivanykha Dub one day with a request that she be allowed to move out and live elsewhere.

Ivanykha was astonished.

"You have been so good to me, Mother-Mistress," explained Mavra, "you and your dear little dove, but the village people have tormented me for too long. They laugh and ridicule me in your mill," and with these words Mavra burst into uncontrollable tears.

"What do you mean, they laugh at you?" asked Ivanykha, knowing full well that the peasants sometimes ridiculed the poor unfortunate, especially when they met strangers in the mill.

"As if you don't know; perhaps you laugh, too?" responded Mavra, vexed. She lit her pipe and puffed at it loudly, building up her courage to resist even Ivanykha Dub. "Every time someone comes into your mill," she said, "they make jokes at my expense. They say 'Will you be milling flour in the mill with your magic formulas for a long time more? Will you continue turning its wheels with your black eyes?' May the power of God smite them," she cursed. "Then again, and this is most grievous, because it is about you and my daughter. 'Are you doing a good job of strewing gypsy herbs around Mistress Dub's house?" they ask, 'so that rich gentlemen will call on her daughter from now on? She, heaven preserve us, is growing up!' And another will say: 'Of course she's not strewing those herbs. If she knew how, she would cast a spell for herself, so that a dark one will arrive from their camp, at least on an old broom, to court her. See, she's already grey, though she still flashes her eyes like a black cat from under the stove!' Just like that, my mother-mistress. And I hear this hundreds of times—and with each year it gets worse. I cannot listen to it any more.... It does you no good either, their babbling about the one who lives in your house and who nursed and looked after your Tetiana. Let me leave your house and all this talk will stop."

Ivanykha was furious. She did not fully trust Mavra, knowing that she had a cunning mind and a tongue to equal it, worse than a wasp; that she was quite capable of cutting off anyone who dared provoke her with an unpleasant word.

"I don't believe you, Mavra," she said, hoping with these words to learn the true reason for her decision. "I don't believe you. There is some other reason why you want to leave me and my child. Better tell me the truth, not lies. You have probably reached an understanding with some gypsies during your wanderings and want to return to Hungary. Is that not so?"

Mavra denied it. She had no desire to return to her people. Since she had not found her parents or her child yet, or even her enemy husband or others of her clan, she would not find them now and no longer cared. She does not want to go back to her people, they had thrown her, a young woman, like an animal from their midst, maimed her future. What she wants is peace and to live in the manner to which she has now become accustomed, that is all.

"How can this be?" Ivanykha Dub was surprised, never having heard such a thought coming from Mavra's lips.

"Just like that," was the answer. She was the only gypsy in the village, on Chabanytsia Mountain, and probably beyond Chabanytsia and the entire district. Ivanykha Dub did not really need her any more, for Tetiana would be fully grown in two or three years and would enter maidenhood—therefore she, Mavra, needed to turn to other work—work befitting a true gypsy.

"What kind of work?" asked Ivanykha once again. Was she not doing work that she preferred to do as it was? Who had ever been able to force her to do what she did not want to do? She lay in the sun and basked in its warmth just so as not to do what she did not like doing, or filled the child's head with fairytales. In the winter she would crawl up on the oven bed, assuring everyone that she was ill—so who had ever forced her to anything?

"That is true," conceded Mavra, as though it pained her to admit it. She had never been forced into anything here and that is why she always came back as if to her family, no matter that they were not gypsies. But now she wants to live alone. All alone— there on Chabanytsia Mountain. There is an empty hut there, right over the steep ravine where shepherds used to live from time to time during the late master's lifetime, in the summer or winter. The meadow where the hut stands has been sold and no one lives there. But the hut still belongs to Ivanykha. So she begs her mistress to let her have it and she wants to settle there forever. And if her mistress agrees and grants her this desire without being angry, she will tell her the truth—she wants to do fortune-telling. Chabanytsia is covered with all kinds of miraculous herbs—poisonous and good ones—whatever one needs. She has used them many times without her mistress's knowledge to put someone back on his feet. She will pick them, dry them and give or sell them to those who need them, and that is how she will live. She knows many, many cures and can tell fortunes better than most gypsies, because not all gypsies understand herbs, fortune-telling or magic invocations. She was taught from childhood by both her father and mother. That was how she was able to make money among the gentry and support Radu ... may he be scattered throughout the whole world.

Living in the mountain hut over the ravine she will always be able to visit her mistress-mother and Tetiana. She will not forget them, how can she!—and saying this she wept. Solitude beckons to her, just as earlier she was pulled to wandering. Living alone there, she will pass on to people everything she knows about cures and fortune-telling. People who would be embarrassed to come here will come to her there. Let people remember that there was once a Mavra. Mavra—the daughter of the great musician Andronati and the wife of Radu Lukach himself. Living here with Ivanykha Dub in the valley, where all sorts of people come to her mill, she has no peace. And they laughed at her, how they laughed! But there, on Chabanytsia, in the peaceful quiet of the forest overlooking the ravine, the peasant behaves differently with a fortune-teller. There she is the mistress. She is at the helm with the strength of her magic, there she will put him on his feet, if she wishes. Saying this, Mavra burst into laughter—odd, painful, derisive laughter, full of secret pride—as though a peasant were already standing before her.

Ivanykha Dub was silent. She was thinking about something and coming to some kind of decision.

Mulling over the gypsy's words, she saw that Mavra was right. There was no need to keep a "vagrant," as people called her, in her house forever, especially since she was occupied with fortune-telling, magic, and other such godless matters against which the priest in church had often cautioned. And Tetiana was becoming a maiden—important people will begin visiting their house—and here they have a gypsy woman living with them.

Still, the whole thing was disagreeable. If she did not let Mavra have the hut on the mountain, she might easily take the child wandering somewhere into the world, maybe even back to her own people. And then....

This idea most worried the grave Ivanykha Dub and contributed to her decision to agree to Mavra's request to move to the mountain hut on Chabanytsia and occupy herself with whatever she wished.

It was hard to decide who loved the young Tetiana more—her mother or the orphaned gypsy Mavra, who had lost her own child, her parents, and her husband, everything to which she was accustomed, and who had attached herself with her entire heart and passionate soul to the child of her kind guardian and benefactress.

Ivanykha Dub would leave her Tetiana with no one else but Mavra. Anyone seeing the boundless, unquenchable love of the gypsy toward this child, whom she had looked after during her childhood and whom she considered almost like her own, could easily suppose, as Ivanykha Dub did, that Mavra could, in her sorrow at leaving the child, take her with her, heaven knows where. That was why Ivanykha hesitated in her heart to resist Mavra's entreaties, knowing full well that she very often made decisions on a whim. And Tetiana was perishing at the thought of losing her dark nanny. She had cradled her from childhood and rocked her to sleep with her sad, monotonous songs that were not known in the area. As the child grew she fed her on various folk tales, which were also unknown and unheard of in the village. It had reached the point where the girl listened unquestioningly to all the commands of her dark companion—to whatever she asked her to do, wherever she asked her to go, wherever she called her. She submitted to her in all things, listened to everything she told her—often against her own mother's wishes.

True, Tetiana is now in her twelfth year, but the gypsy still has more influence over her than her mother. So let Mavra go with God into the forest over the ravine, if this is what she desires, and perhaps then her daughter will slowly, gradually break away from her influence and turn her heart and soul toward her mother, as it should be, as her soul has craved for so long.

Perhaps Tetiana will be more obedient now without Mavra, for she is spoiled to the extreme and not always ready to submit to her esteemed mother's wishes. If Tetiana wants something and her mother refuses her, she flies, sobbing pitifully, to Mavra, who tenderly wipes her tear-stained little face and sooner or later secretly lets her have her way. So it was with everything and everywhere.

Thus far Tetiana's desires had been small, but even with these it was not always desirable to let her have her own way.

Mavra acted as confessor and adviser to Tetiana, and if it had not been for Ivanykha's common sense, she would have taken complete control over the child.

But Ivanykha, despite her great love for her only child, despite the cares of her property, always kept a sharp eye on the relationship between Mavra and Tetiana. Could any good come of it if the girl gets used to always having her way?

Of course not.

Such were Ivanykha's thoughts. Finally she spoke:

"It is not for me, Mavra, to keep you here when your thoughts are elsewhere. Go with God to Chabanytsia, to the hut, and live there as you wish. Come down to us in the valley for food and to help me with my work from time to time. But know this," she added severely, "I will not let my daughter go up to visit you alone. She is all I have. She is everything to me. If you want to see her, come down and see her. But I will not let her go alone."

"Afraid I'll steal her from you?" asked Mavra bitterly, and her sad eyes gleamed at the insult. "Don't be afraid, she is all and everything in this world to me, too. I will not steal her from you."

"You love her, Mavra, but I love her, too. The child is torn between the two of us. You have spoiled her too much. Whatever I forbid her, you allow her to do. That is bad, and you know that we have had many arguments because of this, tears as well. Though she is still a child, she already recognizes no will but her own small, childish will. This must come to an end. Although I have overlooked this more or less here where I keep an eye on her, once she gets stuck on the mountain with you, how much will be left of her for me? Only the fact that she will still be called my daughter."

Mavra did not answer at once, only silently wiped her eyes with the palm of her hand and spat.

"You want her already to have the wisdom that you have," she said, "to be devout and stern, God forbid! But what does she need? A butterfly, a bird, and that is all. Let her play, be happy. Let her laugh and sing; let her have a sense of well-being while she can; let her bask in her mother's love and in the sunlight!"

"I know that she is still a child," responded Ivanykha with her usual consideration, "but it's time she stopped being one. She has been yours until now, Mavra," she added, "you fed her on folk tales, songs, games and everything else; filled her head as if she were a boyar's daughter. Now let her begin to work. She remembers your songs and tales better than she does the prayers I teach her every night and morning."

Mavra's beautiful, dark eyes gleamed proudly and she smiled. "I told her the finest tales I know, I taught her the most beautiful songs. That she is the same as a boyar's child to me—that is true. Is it not the truth—Madam?" she asked. Proudly she continued, "Whose pastures are the best on Chabanytsia, if not Ivanykha Dub's? Whose cattle are the finest, the best fed, if not Ivanykha Dub's? And the beautiful, black-browed Tetiana, magnificently adorned, does she not belong to Ivanykha Dub?"

"Enough, Mavra, enough!" interrupted Ivanykha, frowning sternly. She disliked flattery of herself and her property, for she was modest, devout, and abased herself more before God, perhaps, than even the destitute of the village, never forgetting Him or His holy church. "Enough," she repeated, "and remember: come down from the hut whenever you can, even every day, have some food, do what needs to be done, pamper Tetiana, then return to your hut. And on Sunday, the Holy Day, if I can, though maybe not always, but from time to time, I will visit you with my little one."

"And when Tetiana is grown and ready for marriage, then let her come whenever she wants to," Mavra could not resist adding.

"If God wills that it be so, then she may go. But I will not allow it now. Know this, Mavra," she added, almost pleading, "not the meadows on the mountain, nor the mill over the stream which is my property, but she, alone, is my happiness. I must protect her...."

"No evil will cross her path on her way to me," promised Mavra, and then more boldly: "She'll fly along the White Path from the mill up the mountain like a bird, and then flit back down to you."

Ivanykha smiled.

"What will be, will be, Mavra," she said kindly, "somehow it will be.
Mavra was delighted. Thus it ended.

* * *

Chabanytsia was a high mountain partly covered with ancient forests. Spreading between the forests were the most fertile pasture meadows that belonged to a number of wealthy landowners, among them Ivanykha Dub.

On the mountain, close to its peak and on the side where the White Path trailed and where the pasturelands of the wealthy Mistress Dub shone green, Chabanytsia had hurled out a white rock that people simply called the White Rock. From below that White Rock one could see the entire circle of mountains and forests surrounding Chabanytsia, among them one village, Tretivka, which lay almost on the Hungarian border and was really the third in a row of neighbouring villages.

On the eastern slope of Chabanytsia, a half-hour's walk from Ivanykha Dub's homestead and mill, a white path ran into the forest. It circled the leading into other villages, among them Tretivka.

Following the path from the mill into the forest, travellers would walk between Dub's pastureland on one side, and a steep precipice hanging over a merry creek that gurgled and never ran dry on the other, until they reached Ivanykha Dub's hut behind a number of ancient firs standing a little distance from the edge of the precipice.

The White Path that ran alongside the cottage and fondly encircled Chabanytsia right above the precipice did not actually stop beside the hut. The hut itself was quite indifferent to the path which could, at times, bring an uninvited wanderer to its door. It stood leaning on one side against a boulder, almost as large as the hut, which seemed to have broken away from the great White Rock on the mountain top and rolled its way down to the very edge of the precipice, where it stopped and became a sort of support for the hut. On the eastern side, the hut peered out from under the firs into the gorge with its noisy stream and then further, across it, toward the neighbouring forest-covered mountain. At first glance it was barely visible beneath the wide, wing-like branches of the firs. That is why it was so pleasing to Mavra and gave her the idea of living there alone to devote herself completely to fortune-telling and healing people with the various herbs that grew on the mountainside.

During the first years of its existence, the hut housed the shepherds of the wealthy Ivan Dub; they lived in it not only during the summer, when they put the cattle and horses out to pasture, but often during the winter, if the needs of the farm demanded it. After Ivan Dub's death the hut stood empty for a number of years and only now had a new resident in the person of Mavra the gypsy, who thought that no one and nothing would disturb her peace here. She felt that she could give herself freely to fortune-telling, magic formulas, and all the other occupations that came within the sphere of a gypsy fortune-teller's activity.

* * *

One beautiful summer day Mavra moved into the hut on Chabanytsia.
Twelve-year-old Tetiana accompanied her, together with Ivanykha Dub, as
though helping to carry her belongings which, to tell the truth, were so few
that after two trips everything was in place in the hut over the precipice.

When Tetiana, crying, returned from Mavra's hut along the White Path,
her ears were adorned with the golden half-moon earrings that Mavra had dug
out of her tatters and put into the child's ears as a memento of her.

"Wear them, my child, and never take them off," she said gravely,
fastening them on the girl's ears. "Gold protects from evil and attracts more
gold. I received these from my mother when I was small and she got them
from somewhere far away with her famous fortune-telling. Wear them and
you will always be beautiful and proud, like a Turkish lady."

"Like a Turkish lady," repeated the little girl with equal seriousness,
quietly submitting to her dark friend's ministrations and listening attentively
to every word she uttered.

Then, mutually agreeing to drop in on each other as often as possible, they
parted.

"Come and visit me, Mavra, for I'll die without you," Tetiana commanded
once more before she left.

"I'll come, daughter... I'll come," promised Mavra, silently wiping the
tears that rolled down her emaciated cheeks in sorrow at the parting.

"Every day," ordered the youngster again.

"Well, perhaps not every day," came the answer, "at least not in the
beginning. Because people, seeing me in your home so often, would mock
me, saying that 'the gypsy left by the door and came in through the
window....' But don't worry, child. Mavra loves her Tetiana and won't forget
her. She will come."

And in truth she keeps her word. She visits as she had promised. Not
every day, but not seldom either. Only in the winter is it difficult. Ivanykha
will not allow her daughter out, so Mavra calls on them once or twice a week.
Then, filling her sacks with Ivanykha Dub's gifts and having caressed and
petted Tetiana to her heart's content, she returns, satisfied, to her own shelter.
And Tetiana, who by now has become accustomed to Mavra's absence, turns
to her mother with moist eyes, but smiles and cuddles up to her.

* * *

Mavra quickly became accustomed to her romantic abode and does not regret her move.

She does not miss the village people, for she had had enough of their tormenting while in the valley, for all time. But old women and young wives, girls and boys, and occasionally even elderly homesteaders, both those who were known and strangers who needed advice and cures or magic spells, sought her out in her new home. And none who appear come with empty hands.

One brings flour, another milk and bread, and still another a bit of candle or some coins for tobacco—but each brings something, no one comes empty-handed.

Mavra lives well, she does not have great hardships. She does not need much.

Tetiana, who with every passing year grows taller and prettier, often visits her old friend on fine mornings—and Mavra is not lonely.

During the summer Mavra picks mushrooms and berries, taking them to sell in the town. This always earns her a few pennies. On Fridays and Saturdays she goes down into the neighbouring villages or towns seeking alms among the wealthier folk and never returns with empty sacks.

In the evenings she lays out her acquisitions on the bench and the table left behind by the shepherds and rejoices in them. In the mornings she runs down to her mistress, Ivanykha Dub, to look after some of her cattle—and so she lives, as well as ever before. True, her needs are few. Winter brings short days and long nights that pass quickly. During the spring and summer and into late fall she wanders about, gathering the herbs that she secretly sells, and tells fortunes. Thus Mavra spends her days on Chabanytsia Mountain, below the forest.

* * *

Life is different for Ivanykha Dub and Tetiana in the valley by the mill. Ivanykha is growing feeble from the burden of domestic responsibilities and beautiful Tetiana is growing up and turning into a true forest nymph.

She is now twenty years old.

Tall, graceful and fair of face. One feature in particular, her fair face and its thick, dark eyebrows that arch over her dark pensive eyes, attracts everyone's attention.

She looks like some proud boyar's child, gazing in quiet wonder at everything in this world.

Whoever passes her gazes at her pretty, young face with its loftily-raised black eyebrows that give her face the impression of deep astonishment. Invariably the passerby stops for a moment or two to admire her.

She takes no notice.

She merely looks down in calm wonderment from above (she takes after her tall mother), then smiles shyly. And what a beauty she is when she smiles! The smile on her innocent young lips betrays such a tenderness of heart and soul, such warmth. In addition her soul is pure and white as a dove, knowing no sin. What could Tetiana know of evil when she knows nothing beyond the forest, the mill, her home with its icons and her old nanny, Mavra? But only her dignified mother understood the beauty of young Tetiana. Looking at her at times, she sends up a silent prayer on her behalf. And not only for her physical beauty, but for the goodness of her only child's soul. No one truly knows her or understands her as well as her mother. How diligent, honest, how compassionate she has turned out. Dear God, be merciful to her and grant her a good life!

She is often frightened for her daughter's future, over which she worries, and for which young people lie in wait like true beasts of prey. She notices how people stare at her, approach her, encircle her, at first from a distance, like robbers. Of course, there are nice ones among them, and wealthy ones, but Ivanykha waits and hopes for someone even better, more worthy of her daughter. She does not really know what she is waiting for and because of this seems to be instinctively hiding her, as though for some angel-prince, who is to arrive from somewhere and take her from her mother into his generous care.

Where is he to come from?

She does not know.

Her heart cannot predict this yet.

Not from this valley, or her village. She knows everyone in this valley. She has already refused a number of matchmakers. She did not care for those who were recommended—nor did her daughter. But maybe from beyond that mountain where the stream hides and becomes more powerful, perhaps someone will float in on its waves.

Perhaps....

That is why Tetiana must be guarded and looked after, so that she will not be attracted to someone who is not her equal.

Ivanykha Dub does just that, guards and pampers the girl, hovers over her, and prays for her good fortune.

It will come.

Tetiana is good, diligent and kind—why should God not grant her a happy fate?

An evil fate does not befall the good.

Tetiana lives a quiet life with her mother, like a flower in an herbarium. She does not see or hear much. She knows nothing of misery. She is not even aware of her beauty that blinds everyone like the sun; she only sees herself when she is bending over clear water. And there....

It is said—she sees and hears no one.

Her mother rarely allows her to go into the village to mix with other girls of her own age. The girls live far from their estate and the mill, and she is afraid for Tetiana. She is her only child, like her soul, the heart in her breast. That is why she fears everything. Whomever God has destined for her will come to the mill one day. Its proud hum has sent many their way. It is like a separate world—and Tetiana its noblewoman. Who would not be interested in her, having once seen her?

There is only one thing that Tetiana's mother never forbids her. And that is her visits to the fortune-teller Mavra over the ravine whenever she wishes, and to walk in the forest.

When she goes up the mountain through the forest, Tetiana sings in a loud voice, as if releasing all that resonates in her soul. It is clear, strong, natural and pure. There is no doubt that this beauty was created by a divine hand.

She walks along the narrow White Path, climbing ever upward, from time to time bending over the sad bowed heads of the bell-flowers—among the restless murmuring firs, and always alongside her own and neighbouring pastures. Here she feels a sense of well-being.

And old Mavra! Who can keep guard over the girl as well as she can! Everyone fears her now—if only because of her terrible eyes that can punish with one glance. No one would even dare say a word about Tetiana.

Ivanykha Dub, stern and pious, walks her daughter to church on Sundays and holidays, and in the winter, they ride....

* * *

Young Hryts, foster son of the wealthy landowner Mykhailo Donchuk of Tretivka, near the Hungarian border, learned fairly early that he was not

Donchuk's natural son, but a foundling discovered one morning on the earthen bank outside their front door, wrapped in rags. Though his masters, or, as he called them, father and mother, look after him and dress him in fine clothes, his foster mother, angered occasionally, is capable of cursing him roundly. It is in moments like these that he feels like a "vagrant seed" who has landed in his dusty "gypsy" rags on the doorstep of good people, to torment and worry them under their peaceful roof.

On such occasions Hryts was filled with such deep sorrow and pain toward this entire mountain world that he felt like going wherever his eyes would take him, just so that he would not hear or see anything here again. But it was not only at times like these that he felt a strange yearning in his heart for remoteness ... and some other world. No. This unhappy feeling gives him no rest even in quiet or peaceful moments, will not allow him to remain in one spot, and it is mainly because of this that he incurs the wrath of his foster parents and, at times, even beatings. Occasionally he is put to herding the sheep. He looks after them with care and diligence for a day or two, or even four, then for no reason at all he abandons the flock and drags himself off in a completely opposite direction, where there is neither a decent pasture nor water. Or else he joins other shepherds and their flocks or the lads who tend horses ... and this behaviour continues to repeat itself until he returns home, as if satisfied with this change of scenery.

Once, when he was already a seventeen-year-old lad, he selected the finest horse on the farm and for some reason went off to ride throughout the neighbouring villages. For hours the parents searched and worried for the boy—he seemed to have disappeared without a trace, as though he had vanished with the current. They found him only on the seventh day, leaning peacefully against a hayrick near some horses, without a hat on his head, and whittling a long flute.

"Where have you been, you rascal, where have you been running about on the horse for a whole week?" his foster father assailed him, grabbing his thick black hair and shaking it roughly.

"I visited the neighbouring villages," answered Hryts calmly, at the same time freeing his beautiful head from the despotic hands of his foster father, "I was inquiring about a violin."

"A violin?" shouted the homesteader, his eyes bulging in astonishment. "Is it for violins that I have brought you up and support you, or keep my finest horse for your pleasure? Just you wait, you stupid good-for-nothing, just you wait!" he shouted furiously. "Look at what he's dreamed up, a violin! For shame!"

"Nothing happened to the horse," responded Hryts calmly. "I looked after him and fed him well. Look at how he shines there, well-fed, in the sun. I need a violin and that made me suddenly decide to look for one in the neighbouring village. Father, it's boring to sit around in one place, that's why I rode off. The work I left was not so heavy, you know that yourself, so I went. If the work is urgent, I don't move, when there is none, I go. That's how it is!"

The landowner was speechless, perhaps from astonishment. His hand was again raised to land on the lad's head as before, but he could not. Hryts looked at him with such strangely sad yet sincere eyes, that he only spat, muttered something under his moustache, and left.

Hryts laughed, brushed back his lustrous hair that had slid like silk down his forehead during the pulling and tugging, and set to work again. Father has his ideas, but he has his own, he thought. He very much wanted to find a violin and learn to play it, so that when he was herding cattle or sheep on the summits it would not be so sad and lonely that he would get the urge to run off, but he had no success. Instead he will whittle himself a flute, and when he plays it all the girls at the dances will surround him to listen and weep at first, then dance alone. "Hey-ha!" he laughed at this agreeable thought. "Hey-ha!" What does he care about the master....

But his mother, the mistress of the house, on learning where and why he had dashed off on their best horse and stayed away seven days, approached him differently. Even though she dearly loved him and in her good moods treated him with affection, once she became infuriated, she was implacable and unforgiving.

"You tramp!" she attacked him when he entered the house, and without thinking long, slapped a broad palm across his face. "Tramp!" she shouted again in her quick temper, "you think that God's time is to be spent vainly, frittered away on a horse? You'll remember this excursion," she shouted, waving a hand again to strike the lad, "you'll remember!" But she could not hit him again, for the change in the boy was so remarkable that she restrained herself.

Like a boyar bitten by a snake, Hryts approached her and, squeezing her arm in a pincer-like vise, spoke through his teeth:

"I am not a tramp," he said, his voice low with emotion at the affront. "I am not a tramp. I am your son. And when you deny it, insisting that I'm only a ward, then don't insult me. I don't eat your bread for nothing. I work as well as I know how. If I don't do as much as you would like, then leave me in peace. I'll go away and never return. Get yourself a servant in my place

and it will be better for you. I don't always feel like working, that's why I
don't. And I will not work! You understand? And remember, I am not your
servant. What I have eaten in this house, I have repaid in work," and with
indescribable scorn and anger he slammed the door shut behind him. His
actions and words were so imperious and proud that the mistress turned pale
and was silenced.

"Tfu!" she finally spat and crossed herself. "What is this? Whom do I have
in my home? A foundling, a boyar, or a priest's son? Just look how he
honours his mother—slams the door in her face. And he is not a 'tramp' and
must not be 'insulted.' Mykhailo, did you hear him?" she called out to the
other room to her husband, whose tall, bent figure appeared in the low
doorway.

"Of course I heard" he answered. "So what?"

"What?" shrieked his wife, "you are asking what? Can't you see how he
respects us for the bread and salt we've given him?"

"Why do you keep provoking him with 'tramp this' and 'tramp that?' You
see what he's like, he can't sit still in one spot for a single minute. So what
can you do with him? Kill him for it? I won't."

"I'll teach him," she continued shouting.

"No, you won't. I've tried myself. With anger—and it still didn't help.
You'll see, he won't show up now for a few days. The devil only knows
where he gets his character, but that's the way he is."

"From his tramp parents, I tell you," the mistress nagged him again.

"We don't know his father and mother," the man countered, for in truth
he dearly loved Hryts and always defended him to his wife, although secretly
he himself called him a tramp. "We just found him, a baby, on our doorstep.
He could also be the son of some wealthy family—we don't know. You can't
say just anything to him, he boils up right away, and then it's not easy to
quiet him. Hryts is no tramp to me."

"But I'm telling you that he is some tramp's child. We found him wrapped
in dirty rags, no matter that there was a bundle of gold coins on him."

"Dirty rags or not, he is ours now, so don't be harsh. You can see that he
has no patience. One of these days he'll get so angry that he'll leave us."

The mistress shrugged and was silenced. This had never occurred to her
and for a moment she was disturbed.

"Oh, what a lot of talk!" she said suddenly, in a conciliatory tone, as
though she had had enough of talk about tramps. He'll leave us now—after
we brought him up and his head is practically hitting the ceiling?"

"Exactly now. He can get work anywhere now, he was too young before."

"Oh, what are you saying!" his wife interrupted dryly. "But, Mykhailo, you should know that recently he told me that he has ordered another embroidered jacket made for him. He has already started turning the heads of our young girls."

"Well, I certainly don't forbid him this," answered her husband. "He's handsome, young, so he turns girls' heads."

"He also has to be at practically every dance."

"So let him. The time to dance is when you're young."

"And what if he tells you tomorrow that he wants to get married. The girls cluster around him in a swarm.... What will we do then?"

"I won't allow it, and I won't give him any land. He is not ready for marriage yet—let him first learn how to work on our property, so that I'll know to whom I'm leaving my land one day."

"Ho, ho.... And I'm sure he'll listen to you!" reproached his wife. "I've caught him with Nastia Kryvyniuk many a time. He flirts with others, but he is serious about her."

The farmer smiled.

"I've known that for some time. Her father told me about it himself."

"He would be happy to have him in his family. But I say that Hryts will turn more than one girl's head before he marries," insisted his wife.

"And won't find the right one...," finished her husband.

"And won't find the right one...," echoed his wife, and was silent.

"Old Kryvyniuk is a good husbandman and Nastia is a hard-working girl, she takes after her father. Let them marry some day, if it is so fated," her husband spoke again.

"A *good* girl," his wife said involuntarily, "she already shows the wisdom of an adult. A good girl"—and she stopped.

"She will be good for him *this way*," answered her husband. "He will forget everything for the sake of his horses ... and she will keep an eye on everything. That's how she is good...."

* * *

At times Hryts, who realized from the arguments with his parents that truth was on their side, but on his as well, especially since his temperament led him into initiating these arguments which caused anger on both sides, would leave the house and not return until he had calmed down, and his parents had along with him.

This happened fairly often, and always because of his stubbornness, because he could not tolerate any restraint, took quick offence, and loved freedom above all else. If it were not for the neighbour's daughter, Nastia, who was a good friend and with whom he shared all his woes, or his father's horses which he loved more than anything else, or the sheep that even as a boy he had been able to control with his voice, like children, he would have left his parents long ago and gone out into the world. They keep him here like on a chain, when somewhere beyond their mountains and forests another world and people exist—some people say— especially one grey-haired gypsy who comes through their village from Hungary every few years and stops here to enjoy their hospitality. He will go among them, study, become a rich man and live in this manner, having first learned to play a violin well. Hryts often thought along these lines, especially as a young lad; he would drag himself restlessly from place to place after his sheep and draw angry words from his father and mother. But now that he is a young man, practically an adult, and, as his father jokingly said, "coming close to the age of reason," he seems to have calmed down somewhat. When his mother, angered about something, calls him a tramp, or, even better, a gypsy, he only laughs.

"Do I have such dark eyes and dark skin that you think I resemble a gypsy? My eyes are blue like the sky, the girls say, especially Nastia Kryvyniuk. Because of them I am their darling, but you, who have never seen my father or mother, make me out to be a gypsy. That's a sin, Mother!"

And his mother then falls silent, smiles, and becomes pleasant again; she would have given her soul for her Hryts, because of whom she is envied by all, so handsome and clever is he. No one can stay angry with Hryts for long. He has everyone, so the fair Nastia assures him, in the palm of his hand.

Why?

Perhaps because of his dual nature, or rather two souls that awakened from time to time and struggled for dominance within him. The first one—inconstant, mournful, frivolous, ardent; the second—sensitive, proud, competent. It pulls Hryts toward the good, the beautiful, toward love ... but above all toward freedom that is broad and limitless like the winged forests on the mountain crests, like the swift-flowing rivers in the valleys. Like that wide Hungarian plain that he sometimes saw vividly in his dreams after hearing the tales told by old Andronati (so the white-haired gypsy called himself). He was a born ravisher, a seducer, said Nastia, who loved him like a brother, or perhaps even more, exactly as he was. She was his greatest friend, to whom he turned in his affliction or happiness. Only she brought him to reason.

"Why are you so sad, Hryts?" she asks at times, seeing him serious and discontented.

"My heart is heavy," he answers.

"Then play something for me on your flute or the trembita, play for the both of us" she begs sincerely and snuggles up to him. "No one in the village can play as well, so pleasantly and with such feeling." With these words she takes him into a different world, and to humour her, and himself as well, he begins to play. Here lies his entire happiness, he says—in his flute, the trembita, and in Nastia.

It is true. No one in the entire neighbouring mountain area plays with such feeling, especially on the trembita. When he plays it seems as if he is rushing over the mountaintops like a sacred prayer.

There is not another voice like Hryts Donchuk's as he bustles around the house and the cattle on summer evenings, singing one simple song after another, either a very sad one or a very happy one—he likes no other kind.

All the girls in the village are drawn to him, but he cares for none—except, perhaps, the blue-eyed Nastia. Even then, he will say to his friends, "not always," only when she brings him to his senses, sends him about his work, prevents him from "lazing around." Then he embraces her and assures her that one day he will marry her. Though he chats with all the other girls, he also makes fun of them.

"You girls," he says to Nastia, "are all foolish."

"Only up to a point, my dear Hryts.... Only up to a point," replies Nastia calmly. "We may be foolish at times, but if you should come across one who will turn your head, or maybe even give you some lovage—then beware that you don't lose your vaunted great common sense."

"But I already love you, Nastia," Hryts defends himself, his eyes full of laughter, "and I haven't lost my common sense yet."

"Who knows if you haven't lost it already," she answers, looking into his eyes as directly and candidly as he did. "Oh yes, you say that you love me and you come to me, but then there are times when you abandon me for a week or more to spend time with your horse, rather than with me. Does this show common sense?"

"But haven't I always been like this?" Hryts replies, again on the defensive.

"And maybe you go out with other girls—do I know?" she asks. "I don't know," she says this without reproach, calmly, like a child.

"Well, why shouldn't I spend time with horses or other girls?" he asks, teasingly. "Why don't you get on one of your father's horses, ride with me, and look your fill at how Hryts talks to his horse and enjoys himself with other girls. You'll see for yourself."

"I'm not interested," she answers proudly, hurt to the depths of her heart by his indifference, without showing it. Then glancing into his sincere eyes that for some time have been looking at her with secret amusement, she also smiles, and says:

"Don't laugh and jeer at the girls, Hryts, because the devil himself lives in some of them. Be careful," she adds seriously, "some are beautiful in their youth, they attract you, especially the dark-browed ones, but in their old age, as my late grandmother said, they dry up the cows' milk and fly out of the chimney after midnight on a broom."

"What's that got to do with me?" replies Hryts. "I am not a cow, nor am I afraid of them. I love all of you, both fair and dark, although you are all alike—good, beautiful and foolish—but you, little Nastia Kryvyniuk, I love most of all. And if I tend to forget you sometimes, dear Nastia, don't be angry with me or anyone else."

"As if I were ever angry," she says, looking again with great sincerity and unspoken patience into his eyes. "I've said it myself, you were born a predator and a seducer, that you will never stick to anything for any length of time. I don't say this to be mean."

"I didn't say that, dear heart. You are the only one in the world who is good and generous to me, only you make me see reason, you make me work, turn me back to my home and my parents—without you I would have long ago...," and stretching his arm out like an arc and pointing into the distance, he gave a whistle and smiled.

The fair Nastia is innocently intoxicated by the words spoken by the handsome young man. They mean love, happiness, the whole world to her. At the same time she senses that she holds him by something within her, that she has some control over him, but what it is she does not know.

She makes no attempt to account for this. She only knows that she must continue to hold him, that she loves him heart and soul, and that she cannot be angry with him. Sometimes she thought that if she becomes angry or shows animosity toward him, he will become enraged and fly away like a bird—sit in another tree and be lost to her.

So Nastia is never angry with Hryts. She loves him and hopes her love will always keep him by her side. One day they will marry. Is there a power in this world, she asks herself earnestly, to which Hryts would submit more than he does to her? He loves her best of all the girls, he admits that she makes him see reason, forces him to work, turns him toward his parents. And then? It does not alarm her that sometimes he rides out of the village for a week or two. Her mother says that perhaps this is because he is under some spell, it will pass in time, and she should not reproach him for it. That is why she accepts it all calmly, loves him tranquilly in anticipation of their future together. She knows nothing else. Her generous, simple soul knows only her handsome Hryts, who has two souls. This is her truth, her great, deep, momentous conviction which suffices her and with which she is content.

* * *

It is deep winter.

The forest is restless. The green branches, burdened with snow, have sunk lower to the ground than in other seasons, and the wind that ranges above them and forces itself between them with difficulty drives them to livelier movement. They resist it, but cannot altogether oppose its fury. It rages among them with ever greater strength, then finally lifts itself for a moment above the forest with a wailing roar. The storm has swung into motion.

The wind continues to exert itself ever more vigorously, beating the snow off the trees, rocking their crowns imperiously, humming malevolently, filling the entire pine forest with a sweeping roar.

Now it is terrifying in the forest and dark. And although it is not yet the midnight hour, one can still meet a wolf on a night like this.

Over Mavra's house, hugged carefully on all sides by firs, the pines, as though out of compassion, have lowered their branches that are bent beneath the weight of snow, as though protecting the house from the wind that pressed between them with full force, shattering their habitual dignified repose.

Quiet reigns in Mavra's house. Only the fire in the clay oven crackles cheerfully, lighting up the centre of the room and Mavra herself, who is sitting next to it. She has pulled a wide bench of blackened wood to the stove and settling herself there, is laying out her cards. A black cat lies dreaming, stretched out along the edge of the oven bed, as though watching the fire and the movements of his dark mistress. Beneath the roof over the oven, puffed up and hiding its head under its wing, sleeps a solitary, tame black crow. All the other objects in that smoke-filled hut are sinking into a darkness regulated only by the rise and fall of the fire's flames.

Today Mavra is reading her own fortune. Emaciated and frail, her grey hair dishevelled, she looks like some frightening apparition.

From time to time she stretches out her thin arms to warm them at the flames crackling in the smoke-filled oven, muttering to herself. Her large, dark eyes that seem to harbour a perpetual melancholy from time to time gaze as if in expectation at the tiny warped window, and wait.

Outside the wind is blowing. The coming night seems to be foretelling something malicious, and even though this is not the first such night that she has spent in solitude, it is somehow more terrifying. The wind roars, howling through the forest, carrying on so that even the flames in the oven are agitated. The forest moans and groans as if death himself, together with his cohorts, is pushing his way between the trees. Something is crashing and cracking in the forest, something groans, something is crawling.... Suddenly ... Lord God ... what could it be? Did someone tap on the tiny window at this very moment, or did the wind throw a pile of snow against it to frighten her, alone in the entire forest? The wind is the gypsies' greatest enemy. It likes to do that. It is alive. There are times when it is worse than the hand of God.... She has known this since childhood. The flames dance merrily, illuminating her and the bench, throwing frightful shadows on the opposite wall, lighting up the old, worn-out, curled up cards laid out on the bench, in which Mavra is reading the following:

Misery, sadness, loneliness, to which she is accustomed, but there are also people. Something great and unexpected awaits her, something as yet unexplained. It is still far away, but it will come.

Her dear girl, her Tetiana, is mixed up in all that. She is the only thing that keeps her alive in this world; her "Turkynia,"[4] as she and the villagers call Tetiana, because of the half-moon earrings that she wears. But Mavra cannot understand what else the cards are telling her. Are they referring to her or to the girl? She cannot tell, she doesn't know. She could, perhaps, have explained them to someone else, their days ... or their destiny ... there are none who can do this better than she. But for herself, today, she cannot tell. Does everything that she sees before her predict sadness or joy? For sadness and joy go hand in hand. But here the cards show bloody tears mixed with tears of joy. What does it all mean?

Discouraged, she picks up the cards, lays them aside, lights up her pipe ... and waits.

It is as though she is aching from the night outside. Her heart is heavy—like that of a traitor or criminal. She did not see a single soul all day, let alone have the opportunity to cheat anyone. Who would travel the road into the forest in such weather? Unless they desire death, seek it. Even she

---

4. Turkynia — a Turkish woman.

does not want it yet, she, who does not know why she is knocking about the world. Why go on living? Who needs her? What does she have to live for? She walks in the shadows of life, she will walk until she encounters night itself and unites with it forever....

She mused sadly in this fashion, when something smacked into her small window so that it tinkled, and she nearly cried out in her fright.

Then it was quiet again.

There was still nothing. Only the broad, winged roar and groaning of the forest continued. It was death approaching. In her solitude, Mavra feels as though death is forcing his way through the forest, touching her house, tugging at it with his scythe to remind her of him. Death.

Most certainly on a night like this more than one giant tree would be toppled, more than one tree-top broken, many animals would perish. A terrible night.

Mavra looks about her. Something seems to be missing. Not outdoors, but in her soul, lacking in her heart.... But what? After all, she is accustomed to her solitude.

She wonders.

Her hands involuntarily cross themselves over her breast, but her lips do not move in prayer. She does not know how to pray, she has not prayed, God knows how long. But even when she did, God never showed himself to be well-disposed toward her people. He does not love them. That is why they wander the world in eternal misery. A millennium of punishment. Only at night do they revive. They are drawn to the night, neglecting God, only turning to the moon in their entreaties. The moon helps them, but on nights like this even the moon turns away.

Suddenly the fire blazed up and cast a crimson beam on the bench where the cards lay. Mavra picked them up again, first whispering something over them before laying them out again like before.

Again and again she studies them ... and again she cannot fathom what they are trying to tell her. Something very important and sad and happy awaits her. Something like night or day, something like a wedding, like death. Someone is mixed up in that, someone close and someone from far away. A man and a girl. No, two girls—one good and one bad. On one side, a property and prosperity, and next to that an ancient sack and a beggar's staff. Mavra spits, and shuffles the cards again.

But no, only one thing seems clear.

Two men will visit her house. For one of them—perhaps for him, perhaps for her—death. For the other—perhaps for her, perhaps for him—happiness.

Between the two of them stands happiness. One is young, the other is old. They will both come to her by themselves. The young man—behold—comes directly to her house, though not immediately. No, not immediately. But both are destined to meet in her house … and … Lord God, will one of them bring death along with him?

Yes—death. Terrible, black death. Thus the cards predict—all black cards. Be careful, Mavra! You have sinned during your life many a time, deceived more than once, cheated people who turned to you, trusting in your help.

Once again her mind became confused. Again she is unable to make any sense of it all. She pushed the cards away reluctantly as she would an irksome prophet, a soothsayer—and turning her back to the warm fire, she crouched snugly, bending almost in two along the wide bench and tries to fall asleep.

To fall asleep! One does not sleep on nights like this! Not in places like this. Her shepherd's hut will tumble down, any minute now the white snowstorm will propel it into the deep and terrible abyss. The storm is pushing and pressing down, forcing it to move out of its way, blustering and shrieking. And the snow continues to creep higher up to the window, resting against the wall, blown there by the storm. Only the firs with their thick, sweeping branches watch over her, the sacred tree checking the approach of death. But who will reckon the strength of a blizzard on such fierce nights? Death never roams alone. He arrives with an army, her father and mother told her so long ago. He always moves and flies with an army, flying ahead, with the army following. They always come with scythes, with black banners, always together, and always on nights like this. Lo, how they howl, lo, how they declare their presence!

Mavra begins to doze; the noise of the storm outdoors is slowly lulling her to sleep. But she is awakened suddenly and jumps to her feet, shaking with fear.

Something is beating at her window, seeking entrance.

Death?

Mavra is sure it can only be death.

She throws herself on the ground and crawls to the door, as if to block someone's entry into the house with her body. It is dark by the door, no one will see her there. The flames from the oven are dying down, growing fainter, fading, the room darkens.

"Let me into the house!" She clearly hears an hoarse, elderly voice that sends shivers of fear down her spine and her tousled hair stands on end. Then silence. After a moment again: "Let me into the house!"

Mavra does not move. She stops breathing, her whole being concentrates on listening. Her ears, her eyes and heart—all that lives in her listens.

And she hears:

Hey, how the wind rocks, teasing the firs, reverberating through the trees, the primeval forest. Now her house is rocking and sliding into the ravine, any minute now it will fall apart and be smashed. Drops of sweat appear on her forehead. Death.

"Let me into the house!" An elderly voice again sounds outside. Someone is beating desperately at the door, then falls quiet, without another word....

The house is deathly quiet.

"Let me in!" the terrible voice calls out in despair a third time....

Mavra freezes, remains motionless, as if knowing in advance what awaits her if she opens the door. She cannot bring herself to do it.

A bandit will not show mercy. She knows of many incidents that have befallen people, and even how the gypsies themselves have behaved in past years. They would beg admittance, and when the man opened the door in good faith to render assistance, the blackguard would attack like an animal.... Bam!... and there it ended....

No. She wasn't born yesterday, she won't let anyone in. She doesn't want to be killed. She fears death, she is afraid

"Mavra, Mavra, there is more than one sin on your conscience, do a good deed ... you will be forgiven," something inside of her urges. "Let him in! Perhaps it is a poor person, a stranger afraid to die. Let him in!"

"Mavra, Mavra, come to your senses," entreats something inside of her further, causing her to shake as though with fever. It fights within her, forcing her to the door. It shakes her again, fills her with horror and fearful resistance, as though she has, indeed, heard the voice of death beneath her window, coming as though from the depths of the earth, trying to reach her. She does not know what to do.

She is almost mad with terror, not knowing what to do.

She doesn't raise herself up from the floor, but feels for the door, and straining all her faculties to the utmost, listens for something.

All is quiet outside the window, only the rustle of the pines and some desperate shuffling of feet can be heard, as if seeking a warm spot in the snow, resisting the cold.

Mavra again breaks out in sweat, cold as death, her uplifted arms droop weakly.

No, she will not open the door. She cannot. She doesn't have the strength, her fear is triumphing. Fear in the face of what seems to her to be a subterranean voice entreating her. Let God's will prevail. She is alone in the world, there is no one to protect her, let her at least die a natural death. She cannot open the door. She has hidden herself away from people like a wild animal, but fate gives her no peace even here. Why can't she be left in peace by people, by fate. She will not open the door. She cannot. Let *him with that* voice go with God, *whoever he may be*, good or evil, from far away or near, let him go away. Just as others told her "to go with God" when in the past she searched for her people and begged like a dog at some door for mercy from hunger and cold.

And she went. Whether with God or not, she did not know in her sorrow, but when told to go, she went.

That was why....

She remains silent, immobile, fighting her conscience that urges her to open the door. "Mavra, Mavra, get up," it begs almost desperately, reminding her, "Mavra, open it!"

Her tousled hair again stands on end, again she listens with all her faculties, and again she nearly loses consciousness, she is dying this very minute, surrendering to someone; meanwhile beneath the window, like before, the shuffling of feet can be heard.

* * *

"Two men will come into your house and with them death." The thought flashes through her mind like lightning and she recalls what the cards had foretold.

No, do not open it, her heart tells her. She does not need death. If she survives this night, she will stay alive. The enemy beside her house who has conceived her death and come for her soul, let him go away. Nothing good walks about on a night like this. This she knows. She knows it from her people who only robbed at night, looted and spread misfortune. O-o-oh! Who does not know misfortune!

And again she lies down in front of the door, cringing.

All of a sudden—what is this?

A terrible malediction reaches her ears through the door, stunning her to the depths of her being, turning her body to ice, as though commanding her to perish. Another moment—and again silence. The shuffling behind the door stopped, the voice died away to nothing. It sounded as if the rustle of the forest had yielded to someone, faded away, was silenced.

Mavra is going mad.

In her terror and fear she screamed and fell face down on the floor.

When had she heard this voice before? When? And this terrible curse? It seemed to reach out to her from the bowels of the earth. Whoever received it was marked for death. O-o-oh! When had she heard that voice? When? Mavra, try to remember....

This is worse than death.

Terror and recollection engulf her soul, agitating her to the depths of her being. Is she truly dying? There is no help here from any quarter. She is alone, alone on that whole mountain, in the entire forest.... Alone.... She is dying. Now she knows whose voice it was. She knows. It was her father's voice, the voice of Andronati that had cursed, reviling the offense and disobedience. It was his voice!

Mavra breaks into terrible, manic laughter—laughter that has never before been heard in this solitary house.

Her father's voice? Where had it come from?

From the other world?

Ever since she had given birth to a white child and found herself among the trees in a strange place some twenty years ago, for she could not even remember how long ago, she had no idea what had happened to her father and mother. No one else seemed to know either. She had wandered the world, questioning, seeking. She would return, then resume her search. Before some people she wept as she made her inquiries, but was unable to learn anything about her parents or her poor child. Only death could have wiped out all traces of them. Only death. But this had been her father's voice, come back to her in spirit. Her head is swimming, her thoughts tumble over each other in her fear and the turbulent recollections of her past.

She is certain that it was the voice of her father, Andronati. Only he swore with such terrible, fiery curses that struck fear in everyone. Only he. Both he and her mother had been the eldest of the gypsies. Then how had that curse reached her, to strike at her at this midnight hour? From beneath the earth? For when he cursed at times, the very earth trembled.

She is now convinced that he has come to her from underneath the earth. His spirit has come to announce her impending death. Three times it begged for admission to her hut, and thrice she remained silent, and because she did not go out and let him in, he had cursed her.

* * *

Her father's voice, a voice from the dead. Terrible, hoarse, hollow, ominous. She is guilty! Why had she not opened the door?

She grimaces.

Open it for whom?

It is after midnight and only thieves or the dead walk the earth at this hour.

Tormented, Mavra lies on the floor groaning, calling out to God—praying. What if her father is alive, the thought shoots through her mind, and in his wandering had accidentally come upon her house, and she had not let him in.... Oh God, don't let it be that she had refused her *father* entry. Still, the thought continues to torment her, it could have been like that. He was walking, as poor people usually walk, whether for life or death. Who else wanders like this, if not the gypsies? He had lost his way, suffered cold, and found a path to her light, to a warm shelter. He had begged and entreated.... Oh-h-h! Mavra, perhaps it was your father whom you would not let into your house—and even without that you have quite enough sins on your soul. You have committed an offence! Thus she fought with herself—something kept calling to her, begging her to open the door, but her fear of death would not allow her. She could not, she was afraid.

As time passed she continued to listen, her body trembling. Would he return? But she heard nothing more. Silence, only silence. Only somewhere in the distance the deep, protracted, hungry howl of a wolf sounded through the forest, together with the monotonous rustle of the trees. Nothing else. The fire in the stove was barely flickering, as if winking at the darkness in the room where a deathly silence reigned....

Mavra did not desert her spot beneath the door. She continued to lie there, huddled in fear. Agitated in her terror and thoughts about her father, she suffered until early dawn.

When the morning light began to creep through the forest she rose and went out of the house. In the snow in front of the door and below the window were visible large, blundering, clumsy footsteps that disappeared in the direction of the neighbouring village.

Mavra returned to the house. She could not rid herself of the feeling that she had committed a great wrong in not opening the door. Now, in the light of day, she told herself that the voice that had so frightened her and reminded her of her father could not have come from the dead, but from a living being. She realized it now. The large, agitated, despairing human footprints were here beside her house. And when she had not opened the door, they were lost in the forest and had gone, perhaps, to be met by wolves.

Returning to the house, Mavra built up the fire. What was she to do? Immediately after she began to read her fortune in kernels of corn, hoping to find the answer to what had occurred during the night. Did it bode her good or evil?

She was not successful.

The kernels did not fall in pairs. No matter how she would mix and throw them, they never landed in pairs, always in uneven numbers....

Mavra sat lost in thought.

She sees clearly now that she had done wrong in not letting the man into the house, that it would lead to grief.

*   *   *

Every Sunday when the weather is fine, Tetiana, dressed in her finest, walks through the forest to Chabanytsia above the ravine to visit with her old friend, Mavra.

This Sunday is no exception.

Picking two exquisite red poppies from the garden and tucking them into her hair above the golden half-moon earrings that she had received from Mavra long ago, and because of which the villagers have called her Turkynia since her childhood, she looked beautiful indeed.

And thus she set out on her walk.

Pausing at last before Mavra's house, and realizing that Mavra's door was carefully closed from the outside, she guessed that Mavra had either gone to the neighbouring village or into the forest, as she often did, to search for wonder-working herbs. There was no point in waiting for Mavra's return, for once Mavra left the house, she often amused herself in this way the whole day.

Tetiana followed the White Path further into the forest, thinking that she might just meet the old woman along the way. Walking alongside her mother's pasture, she gazed with pleasure into the deep ravine on her right, along which flowed a cheerful stream that enlivened the entire deep, silent valley, and whose silver path divided Chabanytsia from its steep and forested neighbour.

It is said:

On the right the ravine-chasm with its noisy stream, on the left Chabanytsia, bisected by the "White Path." In places the path is wide enough to accommodate two or three people abreast, then it narrows again into a narrow little snake—as space above the chasm permits.

Tetiana loves to walk here.... On this side of Chabanytsia there is a wonderful echo: if you shout across the ravine the sound will reverberate deeply, as though from a human breast. Sometimes, though rarely, her mother's friends also cross here. Of course, it is out of bounds to complete strangers. Tetiana knows every tree in the area, the flowers, where the finest grasses grow, the patches where the wild strawberries and raspberries are thickest, the quickest way to the White Rock which offers a vista of the neighbouring villages, as though they were in the palm of your hand. Everything here is familiar. Thus, unhurriedly, she descended the very top of Chabanytsia, looking about in every direction, until her attention was captured by the sound of rapid hoof-beats behind her. Astonished, she stepped out into the middle of the White Path, wondering who could be riding here on a horse ... and stopped. Galloping toward her on a coal-black, thick-maned steed was Hryts from the village of Tretivka. Seeing the girl, her head adorned with large red poppies, who had come out of the forest looking as amazed at his presence as he was at hers, he, too, stopped, and they stood there for some moments gazing silently at each other.

He was the first to recover, and, raising his hat, he greeted her.

She answered without moving from the spot where she stood, looking at him with her radiant eyes, her dark brows still raised in momentary astonishment.

"Are you going on?" asked Hryts, and without really knowing why, slid off his horse.

"No," she answered quietly, indifferently, then added, "Go around me."

"Ride around you?" he asked looking at her with surprise, yet unconscious respect.

"Yes. Go around me. I am going no further, neither forward nor back. I have to wait here."

"Why do you have to wait?"

"Because!"

"Are you expecting someone?" he continued.

"Well, hardly today. I'll go home later."

"Do you always wait here?"

"Of course not!" she said impatiently. "It just happened today. I was to meet a woman here and she didn't come."

"So, instead of a woman you met me," he smiled slightly, his gaze not wavering even for a second from her dark, arched eyebrows.

"Ride around me." Again she spoke quietly and, with a hint of pleading in her voice, repeated, "Ride around me."

"But why?"

"Because!"

"You won't move off the path for me?" he asked, with resignation.

"I don't know. Well, maybe. The whole thing is so foolish," she added lightly, and stepped off the path.

"Who are you?" he asks, only now noticing her half-moon earrings, which swung lightly with each movement of her head, accentuating the beauty of her face with their golden sheen.

She does not answer immediately, but looks at him with arched eyebrows, as if with scorn.

"What village are you from?" he presses further and steps closer to her, seeing that she looked as though she might turn away or even disappear into the woods.

"Stay!" he begs, grasping her by the hand.

"Why?" she asks, impatiently.

"Tell me your name!"

"I am *Turkynia*," she answers, looking squarely into his beautiful sky-blue eyes, which she finds somewhat disconcerting.

"Turkynia?" he repeats, baffled, for he has never heard of any Turkish women in the district.

"Turkynia," she calmly repeats and turns away, because she can no longer bear his bright and interested gaze upon her.

"Wait, beautiful Turkynia!" he implores, and instinctively puts his arm around her shoulders. She slides out from his embrace, and again raises her eyebrows.

"You don't know me, and you're pestering me" she speaks dryly and pushes him away with quiet resistance, "Do you think I am available for everyone? *I* am not for everyone! I tell you, *I'm* not for everyone!"

He became serious.

"I see that you are as beautiful as a nymph, and I love beautiful girls."

"There's nothing clever about that."

"And I could easily fall in love with you."

"Just try. Do you think, as I have already said, that I'm available for everyone? No, I'm not for everyone!"

"But maybe for me?" he said humbly and bowed low, holding his hat in both hands as he did so.

"Then go ahead, love me!" she answers coolly, as before, but looking at him with a bright, startled gaze and moving back a few steps.

"You're going away!" he accused her again.

"Why not? Nobody stands in one spot for long."

He fell into step beside her, silent, noticing that she is almost as tall as he is, then asks:

"Your parents are Turkish?"

"No," she answers.

"Where is your house?"

"Where do I live?" she repeated. "Well, as you see, I'm in the forest, so...." She stopped, waving her arm forward, then behind her.

"Somewhere here in the forest?" he presses, not understanding her gesture.

"No," she answers, and suddenly bursts into laughter, so hearty and spontaneous, that he felt he had never heard such laughter before. At this his sensitive nature took over and he became offended.

"Why are you laughing?"

"Because *you're a fool*!"

He flared up....

"You-u-u!" he snaps, and with blazing eyes waves a hand threateningly. "Take care, you wretched girl, watch what you say, for I am not the fool you take me for!"

She holds her head proudly, her brows arched, as if measuring him from head to foot, and drawls out lightly, disdainfully, "You don't say!"

Now he boiled over.

"You!" he says, his voice accentuated with menace that flows through his body and concentrates, like lightning, in his eyes. "You just say one more word like that again and you'll see who the fool is!"

"You don't say!" she dares him again, taking a step toward him.

His eyes burning, he raises his hand, but she bends toward him with lightning speed, facing him with eyes half-closed, as if expecting a caress, her lips smiling. "You're a fool," she says softly, caressingly. "You're a fool, and I am Turkynia, I'll have you know!"

He was dumbfounded.

"You she-devil!" he replies, a deep wave of excitement suddenly overcoming him. "You she-devil! Even if you are a Turk, when I get my hands on you, you won't live to tell it. Do you know who I am? I am *Hryts*, from near the Hungarian border, the son of a wealthy man!"

"You don't say!" she answers, measuring him from top to bottom with her eyes, her dark brows and, it seemed, with her entire tall, slender and captivating figure.

Hryts spat. In his agitation he does not notice the stubborn set of her mouth.

"You're so brave that you're afraid of no one?"

"Whom should I fear?"

"Someone like me, no?"

"Not at all like you."

"Then just look at what someone like me can do!" He pointed to his beautiful horse. "Just watch!"

He turned around, picked up the horse by its front legs, like a pup, and held it standing on its hind legs for a good minute.

"See how strong I am!"

"Yes, I see. But what's that got to do with me?" *Pvrr*

"Everyone in the village knows of my strength. Everyone is afraid of me, and I am afraid of no one."

"What's that got to do with me?" she repeats and moves with extraordinary pride and assurance, walking beside him and his horse.

"I'm the son of a wealthy man...," he proudly persists.

"And I am *Turkynia*...."

"My father owns pastures and a herd of horses, hundreds of sheep, no one has more cattle, and much, much more!" he ended on almost a singing note and whistled.

"Did I ask you?" she answers again.

"You're so ... the devil only knows!" He is angry again.

"My mother is wealthy," she answers. "She has the finest pastures here on Chabanytsia, horses, sheep, cattle ... a mill and rolls and rolls of linen—and I, you *son of a wealthy father* from the *Hungarian border*, am Turkynia. See?"

Hryts gave another whistle.

"She walks around the forest waiting for someone, she doesn't know for whom—like a fool," he added contemptuously, then stopped.

"And meets a fool," she finished calmly, and again lifted her brows and looked him directly in the eye.

He bursts out laughing. "Just look who's stuffed to the gills with Turkish wisdom!"

"I am the way I was born and as you see me. I told you: 'Ride around me.' Why are you bothering me? I am not for just anyone at all."

"And what if I should beat you, right here on the spot?" He gazed at her beautiful fair face with a piercing eye.

"No one has ever beaten me in my life," she answers sadly. "You would be the first, and at the same time, the last to do so. You want to try? Go ahead, beat me! You'll have something to brag about later, just as you bragged about your horse." *Periddd*

Hryts does not seem to hear her last words. He gives her a sidelong look, pulling his moustache. She, too, is gazing at him, but completely calmly, unmovingly. She is looking and pondering something.

Time passes, but neither utters what they safeguard inside themselves, what grows momentarily between them and stills their lips. Tetiana clasps some kind of painful sadness over what had just transpired, while he is deeply moved.

Suddenly she speaks: "Go with God, I am late because of you."

He looks at her with his large, frank, sky-blue eyes. He would like to say something more, but is afraid of her. She is so beautiful, but strange, somehow. He is confused. He has never met anyone like her. Where does she come from? Lord!

Finally he gathers up his courage.

"You don't love anyone?" he asks shyly.

"I don't love anyone," she answers quietly, and saying it, looks at him openly and honestly as she had at first, a little startled by the question. Then she adds, "Do you love anyone?"

"I don't love anyone either," he answers, and as though some of her sincerity has rubbed off on him for a moment, he gives her the same open and honest look.

"As you wish," she says, and again adds gravely, "go with God, I will be late because of you."

He was saddened. Her last words hurt him deeply.

"Why are you in such a hurry?"

"And why should I waste my time standing here with you?"

He gritted his teeth, but did not step aside.

"So, what is your name?" he could not stop himself from asking again.

"I've already told you. Can't you guess?"

"You haven't told me anything, and I can't guess."

"Turkynia!" And saying this she turns from him and stoops to pick up the reins of his horse, which he had dropped to the ground and on which the horse had stepped. She lifts them and throws them over the horse's mane with a sure hand.

"You should take better care of your horse," she remarks, and without another word she turned away, and pushing aside the thick branches of a couple of neighbouring firs, she disappeared before his very eyes....

He stood as though singed by fire, gazing after her.

Where had she disappeared? Where did she go?

She had thrown out a bait, then vanished like the wind....

Tetiana looks at her with her clear, bright eyes, as if preparing in advance to listen to what her old nanny will reveal to her.

"Love—it's like this," Mavra says suddenly, sitting up and folding her legs beneath her. She bends toward Tetiana as if to disclose a very great secret to her. "Like this," she says. "You will meet him once, twice, three times, and maybe more, I don't know. That depends on what each is fated for a certain period of time. Then sometime, suddenly, you will find him at your side. He will draw near to you and you feel that he has already kissed you—one time, a second time, and a third time. He loves you, Tetiana. You, Tetiana, love him.... And why would you not believe him if he loves you?" And here Mavra bursts into such loud, uncontrolled laughter that it makes Tetiana's flesh crawl to hear her.

Tetiana turned pale, not understanding the old woman.

"Sometimes it happens that after all this, he will leave you," continues the gypsy with half-closed eyes, "because he has found another, or else has even had two before you ... so...."

"Oh-h-h!" Tetiana interrupted with a painful wail and, clenching her lips, breathes heavily. She looks at the old woman with pleading eyes, her hands clasped as though in prayer, silent and unmoving.

"Don't expect compassion, my dear," Mavra replies firmly, "there is no mercy in anyone in this world, and least of all in those who behave this way. In any case ... of what use will it be to you? Will it be of any use to you when, after all that, you ask for charity, wander from house to house, but after all—'mercy.' God Almighty, deliver us from this—that we should have no need for it. That's how it is, daughter."

Mavra herself had lived through this.

Her husband had been a gypsy chieftain and highwayman, Radu Lukach, who was wicked as a wolf, sly as a fox, and handsome as a boyar. But what of it? She once danced near a small Hungarian town near the plain in front of people who had come there especially to see the gypsy camp and the gypsies, and earned money for this.

"You danced, Mavra?" the girl asks in wonder, hearing this from the old woman for the first time.

"I danced, daughter. And how I danced. Always around a campfire, and especially when we were visited by lords who came to learn our way of life and customs. Father played the violin, others on the cymbals, and I danced. God, how old Andronati would play!" With these words Mavra shook her head in amazement. "Once one of the lords, a young and handsome boyar, asked me to come to town to tell fortunes and to dance. I went a few times,

---

* * *

His horse lowered its head to the ground where a large red poppy lay and nudged it. Hryts angrily, almost jealously, jerked the horse's head up, picked up the red flower, examined it, then, tucking it into his hat, mounted his horse and rode back.

* * *

The following Sunday Tetiana, deep in thought, braids her silky black hair and, like the Sunday before, adorns her tresses with red poppies and leaves to visit Mavra.

She walks pensively, dejectedly, with Hryts on her mind. Tetiana has thought of nothing else but Hryts. She does not think about the words they spoke to each other, what he said, just about him.

Walking, she looks about apprehensively, even though she knows that she will not see him on this path again. This path belonged to her mother and was rarely used by other people. Those who did were very close friends who had been given permission. So Tetiana is almost certain that she will not meet him.

She is going to visit Mavra today. It is such a quiet, peaceful day! The dreamy firs bask lazily in the summer sun, as if they have become indolent beneath its rays.

Perhaps Mavra will be at home today. Let it be so. She wants to have a talk with her, although she would not mention for the world what happened to her in the forest. This will be one of her last visits to Mavra for some time. For some reason her mother was beginning to look with displeasure upon these Sunday visits. She has not forbidden them outright, but Tetiana understands her mother well without words. Finally Tetiana stops near the hut and looks about. The little house is shut.

Tetiana thinks a moment, then calls out in a ringing voice:

"Are you home?"

"Heigh-ho!" a drawling voice answers from somewhere and Tetiana follows it.

Some four steps past the house, on the very edge of the precipice, lies the old gypsy, sunning herself, propped up on her elbows and puffing at her pipe.

"Mavra!" Tetiana calls out. "Why are you hiding here basking in the sun like a lizard, and the door of your house closed as if against robbers?" asks the young Tetiana, though in truth she feels somewhat ill at ease today, standing before the old gypsy, whose glittering eyes seem capable of unravelling one's very soul.

Without changing her position in the least, Mavra appears to disregard the young girl's words, looking at her with her glittering devilish eyes, and instead of answering asks:

"For whom do you adorn yourself in red flowers every Sunday, precious, surely not for old Mavra? Eh? Just look at how beautiful, how proud, how like a princess she is. Heigh-ho!"

Tetiana blushes beneath this scrutiny, but answers in all innocence:

"For you, Mavra. Who else is there? Today is Sunday. But get up and let's sit in the shade of the fir tree, I mustn't roast in the sun. I've perspired enough from climbing the hill, and I don't want to sit in the sun now. Why have you lain down right on the edge of the precipice? Aren't you afraid of rolling down into its depths if you doze off?"

The gypsy showed her white teeth in a broad smile.

"I'm not afraid. I never fall asleep, and as for rolling off, I won't. Unless some bird of prey dives down on me and lifts me into the heights. But I'm not even afraid of that, for realizing that Mavra is old, it will very quickly release her from its claws. So there is really nothing for her to fear, not even this steep abyss. But if you want to know why I'm hiding on this very spot and closing my door so early, as though against thieves, then this is why I did it. Very early this morning, when I was just finishing my night's rest, those accursed shepherds, hatching some devilish plot, fell upon my house shouting: 'Mavra, the Tatars are coming! Hand over your money, Mavra, the Tatars are here!' They thundered at my door and windows, their wild laughter resounding through the forest, then they disappeared."

"Fie!" she cursed, "the brainless devils interrupted my sleep."

Tetiana laughed heartily, picturing the young shepherds as "Tatars" chased by a dishevelled Mavra.

Silent then, they both sit beneath the shade of a neighbouring fir. When Mavra makes loquacious inquiries about the health of her mother, Mistress Dub, and about her household affairs, Tetiana answers in a distracted manner, unconsciously listening to the foaming stream in the ravine, seeing from where she sat high above it, as though from a tower, how it glitters in its depths at the sun, how it washes the white rocks with its silvery, crystal-clear waters. At this moment the facing wall of the neighbouring mountain, steep and thickly forested, and separated from them by the ravine, is drinking in the

rays of the setting sun which glimmers, slanting down into the green mass of the even firs as if trying to break through them.

"Now there's a real bird of prey, Mavra!" the girl interrupts Mavra's longwinded questioning and points to a large eagle circling quite low above them, as though seeking the best place for itself among the tree tops.

Mavra glanced at the clear blue sky.

"It's circling over you, daughter," she declares prophetically. "Remember, this is Sunday. See that you don't catch the eye of some rapacious lad by next Sunday and get involved with him forever," she says and grins broadly like before, showing her white teeth.

Tetiana blushed furiously.

"I rarely go to dances, Mavra. You know that Mother won't let me go anywhere unless she goes, too. It's like a monastery at home. Our house is quiet, there are only the icons and us in it."

"There will come a time when you will marry," Mavra replies, "so why go? Let those who have nothing go to dances to seek their fortunes. But for those like you, people will come to the house themselves. Your mother knows perfectly well what to do and how to do it. There is no other Ivanykha Dub in the village. It is not for such as you to suffer grief, misery or poverty, my child. Wait for the matchmakers this fall. Your mother told me that she has been approached again."

Tetiana did not reply. She had heard this from Mavra a number of times, but was indifferent as to whether matchmakers came or not, so she did not respond to the words of her old friend.

"Now tell me the truth," questions the old woman, "have you not found some lad to your taste yet? Are you in love?"

"No, Mavra," answers Tetiana dryly, speaking the truth. She truly does not love anyone. Does not love or desire any of the young men she has known for a long time.

"It is for your own good, daughter, and peace of mind that you don't love any of them yet," says Mavra understandingly, "for when you fall in love, you step with one foot into pleasure and with the other into hell."

"I wouldn't know," Tetiana says quietly, her eyes wide and interested, her brows arched, but seeing nothing. The mountain on the other side is, like always, covered with firs from top to bottom, pierced by the slanting rays of the sun and looking exactly as it did before. Nothing else.

"Of course, you don't know, dear heart," Mavra assures her. "That is true, you don't know. But I know," and smiles enigmatically in a way that none can fathom what she is about.

sometimes with Father, sometimes with my husband. There I met the handsome boyar for the second time. He showered money on Radu for the dancing and on me for fortune-telling. Radu, greedy for gold, began sending me out again and again to make money in this way. When I went with him, I danced, but when I went alone, it was for fortune-telling. Though I didn't always want to do this, I had to, because of my fear of him. There I met the handsome boyar again a third time, then a fourth time, until he began secretly kissing my eyes, caressing me and calling Mavra his dark star—until she fell madly in love with him.... My dear!" she added suddenly, cautioning the girl who was growing pale as snow as she spoke, "I was young, beautiful, and foolish; he was rich, handsome as the moon, he rode a horse like the wind. Why shouldn't I have grown to love him when he, a lord, was not ashamed to embrace a poor gypsy girl, call her his star, to kiss and caress her?... My dear! Anyone who has lived through such a love, true, sincere and passionate as young Mavra's for him, then, dear Lord, they ... would take pity on the poor woman who had, after all, sinned in this world," groaned Mavra, throwing herself face down on the ground and saying no more.

After a moment she continued: "Later, when I cried and lamented before him, shaking with fear at the thought of what would happen, and even more afraid of Radu's punishment that would inevitably reach me because I had sinned, he shrugged his shoulders, saying that I had only myself to blame. He whistled at me as if I were a dog, and left the house.... Though I was but a poor gypsy, my child," continued the old woman, "on whom people sometimes sic their dogs, and he was a proud lord who kissed and caressed me, and though I have forgotten a great deal of what happened to me since then, that whistle that I received in thanks for my love for him I will never forget. Never!... I cursed him. But what of it?" she asked bitterly. "He stayed a lord, and I.... I sealed my fate ... to this very day. My beautiful daughter," she warned again, "be on your guard against love! I'm warning you again. Do you think he was punished?" she asked, almost annihilating the girl with her diabolical stare. "He was not punished—only I was. Radu and the gypsies threw me out, killed the child, or maybe even stole it. My parents rejected me and, like a wounded animal, I found myself in your forest. A sacred tree, that one," she added with unusual piety, pointing to a fir, "saved me from death, it brought your mother, and has kept me alive ever since. If not for that, there would be no trace of Mavra by now."

"This is what love leads to, my child," the gypsy returned to her earlier warning, "to this. And this is love!"

"But what's the use in talking," she added, almost in desperation, "what's the use? Everyone knows this. I also knew that one has to beware of misfortune. I already had Radu as a husband, still...," she stopped abruptly, gazing far into the distance with such sorrowful eyes that Tetiana was overcome with pity.

"Tetiana, love sincerely, if love will be your fate," she said finally, in a tone of caution, as though she had recovered from her painful memories, "but don't love behind your mother's back and don't love *two* at the same time. Besides this, beware of *one*, daughter ... of *one*."

FACTS

"Why?" Tetiana asked, almost inaudibly and turned pale as she had earlier.

"Be careful ... take care...," was Mavra's answer, "so you don't end up with a whistle...."

Tetiana's eyes suddenly lit up with something so proud and strong, so spirited and unapproachable, that Mavra was struck dumb, especially since Tetiana, without saying another word, suddenly rose and drawing herself up to her full height, like a fir, said:

"There will be no whistle, Mavra, don't be afraid. No one will 'whistle' at me," and arching her dark brows, she repeated, "no whistle."

"May God protect you from it," agreed Mavra, seeing that the girl was strangely agitated, "may he protect you."

"May he protect me," repeated Tetiana this time, and was silent.

Mavra smiled. Raising herself to her knees, she clasped the girl around her waist and pulled her gently down beside her again.

"May he preserve you."

Tetiana remained silent, as if something had taken away her ability to speak. She could not utter another word. Her head was spinning with memories of the previous Sunday. She tried to smother them with the extraordinary force of her pride. She did not wish to talk about them. Better to slide into this abyss than to reveal that secret by even one word to anyone. She didn't want to—she couldn't.

"He was so handsome and splendid," began Mavra, returning once again to her past, "like the very moon in the sky. A lord, he was. Tall, with dark hair and blue eyes, like the sky, beautiful and sincere—God, how sincere: And a moustache like silk, hey, he-y!"

"Mavra!" the girl suddenly cried out as if returning from the other world, "Mavra!" and again fell silent.

Mavra turned her eyes to the girl with interest, but Tetiana remained silent, her face pale, her eyes wide open and burning like two black stars, the red poppies near her face trembling slightly.

"Oh look, there's your hawk," the old woman spoke up, pointing to the bird which, having rested for a moment on some tree-top, was soaring upward and flying away.

"He's from the other side," answers Tetiana distractedly and pensively, and slowly begins to get up.

"From the other side."

"I'll be going now, Mavra," the girl says, "the sun is setting and it will be dark before I reach home."

"Go, and come to Mavra again," the old woman begs, lifting herself to her feet to accompany the girl a few steps. "And the next time," she adds, "you tell me something, and may yours be better than mine."

Tetiana did not answer. Like a frightened doe she darted through the forest, her heart filled with a strange yearning sadness, running faster and faster down into the valley until she reached home.

* * *

The next Sunday came and again Tetiana is walking through the forest as usual, after spending a little while with Mavra. Taking leave of her mother, who this time had come to see Mavra on some matters, Tetiana continued her walk along the path. Meeting no one, however, she climbed up Chabanytsia and ended up near the great White Rock. After resting there a good while, she gazed down at the villages in the valley, then slowly began to descend. On her way down she saw a rider on the village road along which old Andronati had once carried his white grandson, and which led to the village of Tretivka and wound alongside Chabanytsia and the White Path. She immediately recognized Hryts from the Hungarian border.

But had only her eyes spotted him? Hryts's sharp young eyes also recognized the girl's figure that with light step was descending the hill.

He spurred on his horse and flew like an eagle.

Oh, she recognizes him very well, but is afraid of meeting him. She *would like to* but is afraid of something. She hurries down the hill toward her mother, but realizes that it is too late. He has already recognized her with his sharp eyes. Riding his horse like the wind, he is already on the White Path. Further down the valley, just above the path, he tethers his horse to a tree and is dashing up the hill toward her.

What should she do? Run down faster? asks her heart, hide in the forest? There is no time. The forest begins a little lower and she is on a mountain meadow where the hay has been recently mowed, and he has already seen her, he is hurrying toward her. He will think she is afraid of him. But she isn't, really, but, to tell the truth, she feels very uncomfortable with him. She is not afraid of anyone. So she had told him, and having said it once—she is not going to change her tune.

She stopped just below the great White Rock, her arms behind her head, and looked down at him coming toward her.

He is hurrying, taking long strides up the hill while she stands as though on hot coals, furious with herself at having seen him too late to hide.

"Wait, I'm coming!" he shouts to her, and any moment now he will be standing beside her.

She does not answer, although she is in a hurry—down there, at Mavra's, her mother is waiting for her, and here she is, caught unawares.

At last he stands beside her.

"Turkynia!" he cried joyously, looking her over with his lively, brilliant eyes and catching his breath after his haste up the hill.

"Turkynia," she replies and her eyes also look him over. But for some reason she has turned completely pale.

"Here you are, crowned with flowers like before, and beautiful as ever," he blurts out, not really knowing what to say. Then he adds: "Don't pick all the poppies or there won't be any seeds left for next year."

"Flowers become me," she answers calmly, and continues standing motionless before him.

He falls mute.

She stands high up on Chabanytsia, all alone, calmly, as though made of stone. She is not afraid.

"Hey, Turkynia, Turkynia, where do you get your strength?" he wants to say, but remains silent. Finally he says:

"Tell me now, whose daughter are you," his voice intimating his mastery over her.

"Ask me again ... and maybe I'll tell you."

"Just remember," he threatens, "don't joke with Hryts."

"I didn't call you," she answers. "Go back where you came from. I'm going, too."

Anger begins to boil in him. He cursed through his teeth.

"And who are you?" she asks, without taking her eyes off him.

"I'm a wealthy man's son," he answers. "I've already told you, so that the whole mountain heard."

"A ri-i-ch man?" she drawls, arching her eyebrows as though impressed.

"Rich," he quickly explains in a voice that unconsciously tries to win her approval.

"And I am not your servant," she replies haughtily, and lowering her eyes begins to walk with sure steps down the path.

"I'm not saying that you are a servant," he protests, again with a certain humility in his voice.

"Then why are you cursing?"

"Because you're mocking me."

"I am not!" she answers without stopping a moment in her progress down the hill.

"Take your poppies off and give them to me!" he adds commandingly, and stands in a challenging pose before her. She stops and looks at him, her eyebrows arched in surprise.

"Can't you see that they become me?" she asks.

He clenches his teeth. "I see," he muttered.

"What will you do with them? Adorn yourself, like me?"

"I'll stick them in my hat."

She smiled silently.

The horse, tethered beside the path, whinnied restlessly.

"Your horse is calling you," she says calmly, "walk faster, I'm in a hurry, too."

"The horse can wait and so can you!" he answers imperiously, almost angrily.

"The horse can wait, but I cannot. My mother is waiting for me," she replies.

"*You will wait*," he says firmly, excitedly, "so that I can look my fill at those brows of yours that devils have painted above your eyes."

"Then, look!" she answers, and stands obediently before him, like a child, with her brows arched in wonder as she did earlier. Then, paling, she adds suddenly: "I told you that you're a *fool*!" and prepares to continue her descent.

Again he stops her, this time throwing his hat at her feet.

"Look here," he says, "there are just the two of us on the whole of Chabanytsia. Aren't you afraid?" Something malicious sounds in his voice.

"On this side," she answers coolly.

"On this one," he repeats, piercing her with his eyes....

"And from there," she says. "But at first, when you weren't here, I was completely alone. Why should I be afraid of you? Quickly, tell me what you have to say," she added, "because Mother is waiting for me down below. *She does not jest.*"

He was appeased at her words, as if doused with water, and looked at her wonderingly.

Now she, too, looks at him more boldly, into his large, blue eyes that seem to carry a bit of sky in them and bind themselves to you with their goodness.

"Why do you talk to me like this when we're together?" he asks with an unconscious entreaty in his voice, his eyes desperate.

"Because of how you ask me. Don't detain me any longer, because I'm in a hurry."

He clenches his fists.

"What if I don't want to let you go at all?"

"Then for the tenth time I'll tell you that you're a fool, and you will let me go."

Stirred to the depths by the unconscious firmness of her bearing that he senses, but cannot deal with, he suddenly steps aside and begins to walk with her toward the path.

They walk side by side, both silent in a concentrated, intense silence.

She is pale as a dove, while he trembles with trepidation.

Reaching the White Path, he mounts his horse without a word, without even giving her half a glance; he is turning back. Tetiana is also silent, and without glancing at him, disappears somewhere in the forest, and he sees her no more.

For a long, long time, nothing is heard except the slow trot of horse's hooves which fade away and then the sad, drawn-out voice of Hryts, entreating:

"Turkynia, will-you-come?"

Shortly after, a response, like a bright bell-like sound, like scattered pearls, flies back to him:

"No–I–wo-on't!"

And trembling weakly, as if struggling with the silent forest and the murmur of the trees, the echo answers again, and for the last time: *"No–I–wo-on't!"*

* * *

Returning home, Hryts behaves as if he had drunk poison. He neither eats, nor drinks, nor sleeps; he is sober, but seems incapable of doing anything.

He simply cannot.

He constantly sees before him a pair of dark eyes, dark brows, and two red poppies in bloom, and nothing else.

His father and mother scold him, but he doesn't seem to hear. He listens silently to his just deserts, then vanishes from their presence, going up the hill to the forest edge and the broad pasture where cattle and horses graze. Throwing himself on the grass, he lies there, whether for long or short periods, he is not aware, nor does he care.

Calm and silence is all around him, insects flit restlessly in the sun's rays, sheep bells tinkle softly, the firs rustle in the breeze—and all this accommodates his mood. He needs nothing more.

"Our Hryts has become completely lazy," complains his mother to her husband and he, in turn, will thunder unexpectedly at him. Then Hryts flies into a passion, as if his torpid blood had suddenly begun coursing in revolt against his father, and he snaps back.

"What is this? Am I your day-labourer?" he cries haughtily, retreating with obstinate steps, so that the situation between him and his father will not lead to anger, which yet again will mean having to hear that he was a child fed by their generosity, ungrateful, and other such affronts that give him grief. He mounts his coal-black horse, to which he is more attached than to people, and rides for a day or two, it hardly matters where—into the mountains or over the mountain to a small Hungarian town. It does not matter to him, as long as he gets out of their sight, the quicker the better.

"God knows what kind of blood we have brought up with our bread and labour," his father ponders worriedly. "He won't work, he's not interested in husbandry. He just wants to laze around, live by the labour of other hands, ordering others about! A lord's character, that's what he's got...." He whistles, then falls silent.

But everyone loves him, the devil knows why. He lords it over all the youth in the village, he is the favourite of the girls. His foster son! Ah, Hryts, Hryts.... My future husbandman. Come to your senses soon, so you won't be sorry in the future.

*   *   *

So it is this time, as well.

Hryts is lying near the forest playing long, mournful melodies on his flute while work awaits him. Turkynia is lodged in his soul. She is so beautiful …

so haughty ... so.... Who is she? He has never seen nor encountered her among the other girls in the villages. He still goes to Nastia, to whom he is so accustomed. And although he keeps secret from her what is happening in his heart, he is comfortable with her calmness, her consideration. She never questions or judges, she just loves him. She pampers him, embraces him, and silently he submits to her caresses. Only upon leaving, he might say:

"Thank you, Nastia, for your kind heart. You are the only good thing in my life—some day I'll repay you...."

"Ah, yes, yes...," she threatens lightly, playfully, and adds, smiling: "When you begin courting another...."

* * *

He comforts himself with the thought that he will meet her somewhere again, though he remembers well that she called out in the forest that she "will not come."

"But, maybe...," he thinks, "maybe she will come at least once more." The last time, God knows why, she came into the forest with her mother. But maybe now some other reason will bring her again. Just once more. Just once.

It is not in Hryts's nature, however, to wait or worry for long.

Two weeks later he tells his father that he is going to the neighbouring village for a "minute" to look at a friend's sick horse, and that he will return toward evening.

"Go," his father agreed, and he rode off.

Riding for some time over the narrow, pebbly village road, he suddenly notices the White Path that girds the western side of Chabanytsia and winds down, joining up with the village road like a small stream. His horse is clever—without being guided by Hryts he turns off the village road onto the White Path, upwards over the ravine. He trots along diligently as if proud of his handsome rider, then slows his pace. A little further on, the path disappears into the forest.

They ride on, then stop suddenly. The White Path still beckons before them, but where does it go further on, Hryts asks himself. Where does it come from? Whom does it belong to? He has never travelled far over it, he does not know it well. Does it lead to the third village from theirs, to Tretivka? Or maybe only to some mountain pasturelands? Perhaps she lives in that village on the other side of Chabanytsia? Hey, Turkynia, answer—is that where you live?

Everything is the same. There to the right, high up on Chabanytsia, right above the White Path, hangs the great White Rock where he last saw her. Maybe she'll be coming here again. On the left—the abyss of the ravine, she won't be coming from there. Beyond the ravine is the wall of the neighbouring mountain—she won't be coming that way either.

He does not go any further. There is no reason to; if she were around, she would be here.

The path is probably narrower further up and there is no time to investigate. Better to stop here and wait for her. Thinking this, he dismounts, ties his horse to a small tree to the right of the path, then lies down beside the horse to wait. If she appears along the White Path going toward the White Rock as she did the last time, he will be able to see her immediately. She will be coming toward him, unless she is going down into the ravine. But why there? One way or another, he will see her.

The horse grazes the grass beneath its feet, and he lies there on his side, across from the path, almost on the edge of the ravine, his face turned up the path toward the forest. He will surely see her coming down the path toward him as though down stairs, step by step out of the forest.... Hey, Turkynia, I'm here!

He waits....   *Ig that's love at first sight*

The forest rustles softly.

The wide-winged branches of the firs barely sway. They whisper something to each other, exchanging secrets, assuming a ceremonious stance, as though they are celebrating.... Down in the ravine, in its very depths, the river also gurgles as though murmuring something to itself....

Lying in wait, Hryts looks about, his sharp young eyes missing nothing, like a hawk gazing down into the very depths of the forest. He waits patiently, listening attentively for the sound of footsteps and is finally rewarded. Straight out of the forest, down the path toward him, perhaps only some two hundred steps away, and walking with a light step without a sound ... alone, all by herself, she is walking.

"Quiet!" the trees around him seem to whisper and barely sway: she is coming.

Yes, truly—*she* was coming.

She looks neither to the right into the gorge, nor to the left up Chabanytsia with its White Rock, nor ahead to where he lay like a snake curled beside the pathway. She is looking at her feet as she descends. She is dressed splendidly in a silk skirt, her waist, supple and slender as a reed. Her face glows between the red poppies, the large poppies, under which shine the golden half-moon earrings.

He wants to shout, but is afraid. She might disappear at once. His heart beats loudly.

He lies there without moving.

But finally he must. He stands up, doffs his hat, and bowing low, almost touching the ground with it, he walks toward her, bent over humbly.

"Turkynia!"

She had seen him earlier than he thought, recognized the horse, guessed in her heart.

"You're here?" she asks, her eyebrows raised in wonder. She is still the same as before, he already senses.

"A good day to you, Turkynia, since that is what you call yourself," he begins, straightening up in front of her. Perhaps she will be different today, at least.

"I have come to see you," she says simply, looking him in the eyes, but again pale to the lips.

He fell, bowing as if to a princess.

"Don't bow so much to me, once is enough. Only my mother receives that many bows. They call her a lady."

"And you?"

"I am called Turkynia!"

"Why that?"

"Because of these," and she gestures to the gold half-moons in her ears, "Turkish earrings."

"Who christened you this way?"

"The people in the village. Haven't you heard about me?"

"No."

"Have you never been in our village, in B…?"

"I have a few times, but generally I go more toward the Hungarian border. Once I was at a feastday in your village, but I didn't see you."

"As if you'd remember," she says, smiling.

"Why are you laughing?"

"Why not?"

He was offended.

"Take care," he says, frowning, "that sometime people don't laugh at you."

"Not at me," she says confidently and proudly.

"You don't say!"

She ignores this.

"I believe I've heard about you," she says instead, "but I never saw you and didn't know your name."

"Hryts," he supplies.

"You've already told me that," she answers, "but your village is large and many people have that name."

"*Hryts..., Hryts...*," he repeats, thumping his chest. "The one who has all the girls after him, who dances as though writing with his feet, who plays the trembita better than anyone in the village ... *that Hryts.* This winter I just might come to your village," he adds. "One of my friends has an uncle there and he sent him a message that he should come and visit him, because he has a fine and pretty girl for him. So beware...," he threatens, a smile hiding behind the black moustache that adorns his face.

She raises her dark brows in amazement at his words.

"Don't worry. We'll love one another."

She is silent a moment at this, then asks:

"Do you also leave the girls you've stopped loving with a whistle?"

"So what," he answered, "Should I cry? I might cry for you, though, because you're so beautiful!"

She gazed at him, her eyes wide, then unwittingly pulls the red poppies out of her hair and lets them fall to the ground.

"And what do these girls do, those whom you've left with a whistle?" she continues, staring at him accusingly.

"Well, am I supposed to teach them?" he replies. "They have their own common sense, just as I have. Nobody teaches me, I have no schooling."

"They probably wander the world," Tetiana says thoughtfully, quietly.

"Don't worry about them," he consoles her, and stepping closer, looks tenderly into her eyes.

"You won't be whistling after me!" she suddenly announces, firmly and decisively, but at the same time melting and losing herself in his gaze.

"Not at you," he assures her. "You are my little cuckoo."

"Oh, you!" she says suddenly, gloomily, stretching her arms out against him so that her palms are pushing against his chest. "You!" she repeats, then: "You know what?"

"I know," he answers, his eyes filled with laughter. "You are beautiful as a boyar woman, and I love you!"

"You don't say!"

"You don't say?" he repeats questioningly, and his voice was pierced with anguish.

"Oh, Turkynia, Turkynia," he adds, threatening with both his voice and eyes, "you are lucky that you're beautiful, or else...."

She raises her hands to her ears and only then realizes that her poppies are not there.

"There they are, on the ground," he says with some humility, hoping to win her sympathy.

"They fell off by themselves?" she asks herself, her eyes never leaving his.

"You are so beautiful," he continues, "that I love only you."

"Oh-h-h!..." she cries woefully, bending down to pick up the red flowers.

"You don't believe me?"

"What should I believe?" Again she arches her eyebrows.

"That I love only you."   *Liar*

"Me?"

"You."

"You're handsome, too," she says simply, "but my heart is heavy."

"Why?" he asks candidly, embracing her suddenly, "my heart isn't heavy." She pulls away.

"With you, my heart is heavy."

"With me?"

"Yes. I came to tell you that I won't come any more."

"Then I will come," he answers.

"Where?"

"Everywhere. Wherever you may be."

"You can't come everywhere."

"I'll come, once I've said it."

"To my home, too?"

"To your home, too. Where is your home?"

"By the mill over the river. Do you know where that is?"

"To Ivanykha Dub?" he asks in surprise. "There?"

"There. She is my mother."

"She's a proud lady," he answers, almost whistling, "she bites from afar."

"My mother is devout, she does good deeds for people, she loves truth alone."

"What of it?"

"Nothing. It's quiet in our house, there are only the two of us and the holy icons; it's lovely like that and pleasant...."

"She'll put you in a nunnery yet," he quips.

"Maybe she will, if I should ever want it."

"If I don't marry you."

She blushed.

"Will you marry me?"

"If I want to, I will."

"You don't say!" he mimics her.

"I do say!" she answers haughtily, without looking at him, then quietly adds, "Go!"

"I'll go when I want to, you can't tell me what to do, even if you are a Dub."

"It's much better for me if I don't see you," she said, her eyes lowered and with these words she turns and starts to walk away.

"Turkynia," he shouted in distress, imploring, and reaches her in a moment, "my little cuckoo!"

"You want to whistle?" she asks, piercing him with her large, questioning eyes, as if in warning.

"Turkynia!"

"Go away," she almost begs. "I'm full of melancholy, sadness. I feel a hundred times better when I don't see you, Hryts! Do go—go away! I feel terrible.... Go!"

"You're foolish!" he bursts out.

"You think I'm lying?" she asks, and coming close to him, she looks at him with large, sincere eyes set in her pale, ravaged face, adding: "And don't wait for me any more, because I won't come."

"Come, do come, my little cuckoo!" he humbly implores, bowing low to her. "Please come and coo a bit in the forest, and I'll be waiting here."

Before he realized what was happening, she turned quickly away from him, and without once looking back, parted the branches of the firs and took flight like a bird, disappearing as if she had never been.

He did not have the courage to follow her. He thought of her mother, the lady, and did not want to antagonize her, so he stayed where he was, then turned to his horse, put his arms around its neck, and sighed. He stood there a moment, and without thinking, gave a long, slow whistle.

He listens....

A very soft, barely noticeable rustle sways the air, as if commanding silence.... All is quiet, waiting.

"I wo-on't co-ome!" the sound floats down to him from somewhere above in a wavering voice that he so loves. In its wake came the echo, reverberating from across the gorge, clearly but faintly: "I wo-on't co-ome!"

She sped down the path to her home. Breathless and agitated she throws herself in front of the icons and begins to pray:

"Lord, but I'm sad," she laments, holding back her tears, "Lord, I'm so sad.... Why am I so sad?"

* * *

Riding home in great haste, Hryts goes straight to the fair Nastia. He wants badly to be embraced, find sympathy, tell someone about his love for Turkynia—that she is such-and-such, that she is so-and-so—that his heart aches ... that she had said this ... answered that ... and a great deal more that is boiling inside him. That is why he went.

Nastia was waiting. She was waiting, like always.

She always waited, even if Hryts didn't come, and continued to love him. In spite of everything, she was always delighted to see him.

"Nastia, my dove!" he says sadly, mournfully, embracing her, "Nastia, I'm so tired."

Nastia caresses and pampers him. Nastia is accommodating, she doesn't ask questions. Whatever he wants, she silently carries out, always kind, always loving.

They sit together side by side without talking.... The silence itself speaks for them.

He gazes pensively before him at the forest and mountains and sees nothing. Looking at him are dark eyes, below arching, wondering brows, a face framed in burning red poppies, trembling golden half-moon earrings, red lips like flowers.

"Turkynia," his grieving, agitated heart pleads silently, "Turkynia, why don't you love me?"

"I wo-on't co-ome!" replies the beloved voice and fades into the melancholy depths of his parched soul. "I wo-on't co-ome!"

"Kiss me, Nastia!" he asks suddenly in a firm, demanding tone and pulls the chubby-cheeked, docile girl into his arms, "kiss me!"

She kissed him.

"Like that," he says, satisfied, and, getting up, departs without so much as a backward glance at the girl.

* * *

The red poppies with which young Tetiana had decorated her hair all summer shed their blossoms. The days became short, wet and gloomy. Semi-darkness also reigns in Ivanykha Dub's home, situated between the mountain and the noisy river. The firs that march in front of the house in dense rows up the mountainside screen it from the sun; in the house of the devout Ivanykha Dub a small light glimmers as usual in front of the icon of the Virgin Mary.

The autumn days are dull and tedious for the beautiful Tetiana. Her mother, busy with household affairs and the mill, spends little time in the house whose rooms Tetiana has hung with embroidered towels, decorative wall hangings, and dried flowers. Sometime she doesn't know what to do with herself. It seems to her that she has too much spare time on her hands. Though she helps her mother in her tasks, concerns herself with them together with her, there are still moments when she feels she has too much free time. Ivanykha Dub refuses to allow her only daughter to perform heavy, physical tasks, and her yearning for Hryts and secret love for him undermine her peace of mind and stability. She would have flown up the mountain like a bird toward him; he had called, entreated her to meet him again in the forest—she had not gone. Something that was stronger than her kept her at home in the valley, did not allow her to make this move.

She wanted to see him—but did not go. She loved him—but would not admit it. She closed her heart and seemed to be waiting for something, as if afraid to love as only she could.

"So what, you want me to cry?" The words rankled in her soul whenever she recalled their conversation about girls in love, who should use their "common sense."

Yes, she, too, has common sense, and she did not go into the forest to meet him. She didn't trust him. Look at what had happened to poor Mavra whose life had been wasted—everyone had abandoned her. She had no one in the whole world except her mother and her. She didn't want this to happen to her. Better not to love if it would end by his forgetting her, ridiculing her for having loved him, for losing her heart to him....

While she yearns for him, at the same time she is frightened. No matter how much she prays, she has no trust in him. He will love me, then leave me, ridicule me and he'll whistle at that, her heart warns. So Mavra had taught her and she trusts Mavra. *Yep*

"Oh-h-h!" The very thought of it made her groan, and if there had been trust for a single moment, it had fled without hope and did not return. The thought is unbearable. It unsettles her, gives her no peace, makes her unhappy, consumes her soul. She—Tetiana Dub—abandoned to ridicule? She, whom her mother preserves like a flower in a frame, honoured and loved, who ensures that she has everything her heart desires? She would be abandoned and he would go off whistling! As though beneath a great unseen burden of some incomprehensible fear, Tetiana bends, suffers, and swoons in her love.

So often, so frequently. This is why her closed lips are proudly silent, confessing to no one the pain and bliss in her heart. If he should come or send matchmakers on his behalf, she will speak, she will declare everything. But if this should not happen, it will die with her.

On some days Tetiana melts like the spring ice. She smiles often, happy in heart and soul. He loves her! He is handsome and proud, like an eagle in flight. But he loves her, pines for her. Oh, Hryts, Hryts! Her young soul yearns, spreading wide its pure wings, trembling with hope, smiling in happiness. When will he come himself?

Himself!

Come on his precious steed, black as coal. He will come, kiss her, stand before her mother, say what is necessary, proclaim her happiness.

But Tetiana does not hurry into the forest to meet him, she rushes to Mavra.

Should she tell her? Explain? She is uncertain. Tell Mavra? Betray herself? Or would it be better to remain silent until the right moment....

No, better to say nothing. She must not betray herself with a single word. Better to wait alone, look forward to her happiness quietly, keep her love a secret. In time he will send matchmakers, and all will be well. Her mother will permit her to marry him. They love each other and she will beg her mother to allow their marriage.

But Tetiana does not hurry to meet him, she hurries to Mavra.

She will not tell Mavra about her love, but Mavra knows much, she is an authority on everything, has experience of the world, knows how to tell fortunes, she mentions love occasionally ... she will make her feel better.

While walking through the forest one day thinking such thoughts, she turns in the direction of Mavra's house and soon is stepping over its doorstep.

"Mavra," she calls out animatedly, "even though it isn't Sunday, I've come for a visit. It's so dull and miserable at home sometimes that it almost forces me out, at least to visit you," and saying this she hugs her old friend, as though she hopes for love and caresses in return.

"Mavra, look, I'm here ... so how about a hug and a kiss...."

"What a good story!" answers Mavra, but obliges by hugging and caressing her beloved ward.

"Why haven't you come to see me?" she asks, "have you forgotten Mavra? Are you in love with some lad? Tell Mavra everything, everything that you know. She has only Tetiana, only her in the whole world. Whom else could she love? Who worries about an old woman with nothing but forest around her, forest and mountains. Just this morning those boys were shouting again. The wicked creatures rushed my house again, shouting: 'The Tatars are coming!' They banged at the door and before I could climb down off my perch on the oven, they disappeared. Whom else should she love, fondle and caress, if not her little white cuckoo?"

Tetiana laughed.

"Frightening you with Tatars again?"

"Yes, they flew in from somewhere and started hitting my door. 'Open up, Mavra, because the Tatars are coming!' They left me no time to get at them, except perhaps to curse and hide my herbs so they wouldn't scatter them about."

"Have you picked many herbs this summer?" asks Tetiana, looking into the nooks and corners where her old friend habitually stored her dried, wonder-working herbs.

"Enough."

"What kind of herb is that on your oven?" asked Tetiana with interest, "I've never seen it here before, I don't know what it is."

"*Those herbs*?" asks the old woman dryly.

"Those ones, what are they for, Mavra?"

"*Against all misfortune*," replies the old woman dryly once again. "It's from below the White Rock."

"Against what kind of misfortune, Mavra?" insists the girl, looking closely at its leaves.

"Against *misfortune…*," she hears the same answer. "Give it in a drink and it will overcome misfortune. You'll fall asleep and it disappears. It puts you to sleep," she added more amiably. "If you can't sleep at night you boil it, drink it, and without any trouble you fall asleep. Maybe my enemies fed me this herb the night they decided my fate and threw me out of the gypsy camp. I was carried sleeping from my tent and heard nothing. Some of my people know a lot about herbs. They also know which incantations to use with them. Hey, hey, it's some herb!" she smiled queerly. "Mavra knows all about it, too. Just don't prepare it for yourself, my dear," she warned, "unless it's for some terrible enemy, and be sure you know when it's supposed to be dug up."

While explaining the effects and strength of the herb to Tetiana, she also seemed to be hiding something from the girl, who did not question her further.

"When do you it dig up?" she asked.

"When?" repeats Mavra, "listen, I'll tell you how and when, just don't forget. I won't tell you again. This is only for yourself, if necessary, but keep it a secret. Pour water over it before sunrise, all by yourself, with no one around, and don't touch the pot. It must be done in silence as well. This if you're preparing it for yourself. But against misfortune—it's done differently."

Tetiana smiled.

Mavra began to scold:

"Don't laugh, girl!" she said, seriously, "just remember well what I'm telling you. Maybe I'll die and you alone will remember! Why shouldn't you know? Even though it may not be useful to you, it's a good thing to know. Now then, against misfortune.... Dig it up on a Sunday morning, wash it on Monday, cook it on Tuesday, and on Wednesday it is ready to drink. Then hey-hey, what a sleep to catch misfortune unawares!" And she almost sang these words, shaking her fingers: "Hey, hey!" And she burst into laughter.

"Ah!" she said finally, with regret, "if only I had had this herb with me when he told me that I alone was to blame and then whistled. Mavra would not be alone in the forest today, or in this world. I would be among my own people with my child.... Yes," she added bitterly and broke off.

"Then what, Mavra?" asks Tetiana, her eyes suddenly wide with anxiety.

"Then he would have slept at least three days, if nothing else...."

"Mavra!" cried the girl with repulsion, her brows knitted together in anger, "what you're saying is a sin!"

"Maybe it is a sin," agrees Mavra firmly, "but to ruin me, a young woman, and cause a falling-out with my husband, that was also a sin."

"Mavra, you loved him?" Tetiana replies, an unconscious note of defence in her voice, yet she does not understand why the one she loves, Hryts, suddenly comes to mind.

"I loved him to my misfortune and my grief. It's true, I loved him. He was better than Radu. But what did it bring me? Now I have neither him, nor my child, nor Radu, nor parents—no one, Tetiana, no one," she adds sadly. "Daughter, what do you know about sorrow in a woman's breast? It knows no limit.... May God preserve you from such an experience, even from a distance. You would go mad," warns Mavra, and fills her pipe.

"I would go mad," repeated Tetiana softly and was silent, her brows knitted together in a frown as before. At last, standing very close to the old gypsy, she says:

"Mavra?"

"What, my daughter?"

"You know so much...."

"Well, not so much, but what I need to know, I know."

"Then tell me, are they all the same as *that one* was?"

"Which one?"

"The one you loved, and who loved you ... who betrayed you and whistled when he left."

Mavra looks at the girl as if at a small child and, squinting her eyes, answers:

"Perhaps only one who is born this very minute will not be that way."

At these words Tetiana wilted. She sits down on the bench without a word, and asks no more questions.

Mavra, however, does not remain silent.

"Daughter!" she says, looking closely at the girl, "Why have you been forgetting old Mavra lately, huh?"

Tetiana clenches her teeth.

"You don't love her any more?"

"Of course, I do."

"You haven't started loving anyone else, have you?" she asks, puffing at her pipe, her eyes raking the girl's pale face.

At this question something bursts in Tetiana. She proudly lifts her head, which until now had always bowed obediently to the old woman's will, humbled itself as before an invincible black power that tried to dominate her.

"Well, what if I have?" she asks suddenly, looking fearlessly straight into the old fortune-teller's eyes."

"Then don't believe him!"

"And what if I should?"

"Then don't complain afterwards!" Mavra pronounced the last word almost as a threat.

"I won't be sorry."

"Has he sent matchmakers already?" asks Mavra, once again eyeing the girl closely.

"He will send them."

"Someone from our village?"

"No."

"From far away?"

"I don't know. I know nothing."

"And you love him?"

"I love him."

"You say he'll marry you?"

"He'll marry me."

"When?"

"I don't know."

"This fall?"

"I don't know."

"Tetiana!" Mavra warns sternly, grimly shaking her finger, "Tetiana!"

"What?" The young girl resists something that she hears in old Mavra's voice.

"Be careful, Tetiana."

"But he loves me!"

"And you love him?"

"I love him."

"And he's not from our village?"

'No, not from our village."

"Does your mother know about this?"

Tetiana became angry. The very thought of someone opposing her love for Hryts makes her rebellious. She stamped her foot as she had in childhood when she didn't get her own way, and turned away in fury.

"Ugh!... Mother!" she cried in exasperation, "why should Mother know? He will send matchmakers in time and then she'll know. Now she doesn't need to."

"But what if someone else sends matchmakers before him this fall?"

"I won't accept," she answers firmly and haughtily.

"But what if your mother does?"

"Mother won't force me."

"What if she insists?"

"Mavra!" The girl threw herself at the gypsy in indescribable rage, as though she wanted to strike her, her eyes flaming, "Mother wouldn't force me!"

"No, no, daughter," the gypsy soothes her, in dismay at the girl's fury that reminds her of her childhood tantrums. "Mother won't force you."

"You'll help me, Mavra?" Tetiana implores insistently.

"I will help, daughter. I'll persuade your mother."

"Before he even sends his matchmakers, Mavra?"

"Before he sends them."

"Even if others come and Mother tries to force me?" asks Tetiana persuasively, trying to guarantee Mavra's help from the present day.

"It will be as you say, child. But don't worry. It isn't time to worry yet."

Tetiana sits down by the clay oven where a few coals are smouldering and is silent.

"Is he a rich man's son, at least?" asks Mavra after some time has passed.

"Of course," answers Tetiana with pride, her voice warning her old friend in advance against asking another question.

"Is he handsome?"

"We-e-ll!" answers the young girl emphatically raising her eyebrows, then adds: "Probably only yours might have been like him, Mavra."

"May God preserve us if he should be like him!"

"I said handsome, Mavra."

"I hear you, child," answers Mavra, shaking her head sadly. "That's what led to my ruin," she adds in a soft sing-song, "I gave him my soul—for his eyes."

"For his eyes...," repeats Tetiana dreamily.

"What is his name?"

Tetiana hesitates, then waves a hand carelessly and adds indifferently:

"I met him only once...."

"Once? And already fell in love?"

"Once, twice, three times, and I fell in love on the fourth." *Exactly*

"Secretly?"

Tetiana bows her head and does not answer.

"At the mill?" pries Mavra, trying to uncover the girl's secret.

Tetiana nods at first, but then contradicts herself:

"I don't want to tell you the truth."

"Tetiana," warns Mavra, pleading, "tell him to send the matchmakers, stop meeting him alone."

"He'll send the matchmakers himself," replies the girl resolutely.

"God help us. And be careful, Tetiana! Because he who loves, my child, sometimes destroys," she added prophetically.

"Destroys," Tetiana repeats after her in a barely-heard whisper, and then falls silent.

It was still, silent.

Mavra, deep in thought, puffs at her pipe, while Tetiana once again fights a silent battle within herself, then throws herself at Mavra, presses up against her and pleads:

"Mavra, are all of them truly like the one you told me about?"

Mavra answers firmly, like a stone that falls into the water and is seen no more:

"Perhaps only one who is born this very minute will not be like that."

"Mavra!"

"My dear child, if you have never believed Mavra before, believe me now! You are all I have in this world...."

"He has such sincere eyes … and I love him," the girl answers, as though struggling with her old nanny's distrust.

"You love him, child? Love?" retorts Mavra, "Then love him in happiness, because on this entire mountain, in this entire forest, I am completely alone, both far and near, I am alone, all alone."

* * *

Tetiana walks home through the quiet autumn forest, her mind in a turmoil. She will not visit Mavra any more. It hurts her to know that Mavra will talk about *them*, and about him, whom she does not even know.

She will not go back. She is unhappy with Mavra. No matter what topic you broach, she always casts a shadow on it. But she is in love. She knows Hryts, and he loves her. They know what is good for them.

She patiently awaits his matchmakers at her home, even praying at times. One day he will ride up, her heart tells her, his black steed will whinny, and he will enter their house. He will remove his hat, as he did more than once in the forest, and bowing respectfully, will say: "I have come, Turkynia! You alone I love, you alone in the whole world!"

Wherever she goes, whatever she does, her heart sings one and the same song: Hryts loves her, and she loves Hryts.…

The autumn days pass slowly, one by one, winter is coming—finally it arrives—white, pure and frosty. Downy hoar-frost bends the pine branches and a thick blanket of snow has covered the White Path. Wherever one looks, the entire forest has turned into a white dreamland for a time.…

* * *

From under the thick growth of firs weighed down by white snow, right over the gorge, transparent blue smoke from Mavra's chimney curls upward like a snake. Mavra is passing the winter.…

* * *

For young Hryts the fall and winter drag slowly. At first he would ride out, hoping to meet the beautiful Turkynia, but he soon realizes that she is keeping her word, that she "will not come," as she promised she would not. He is saddened, thinking that if she really loved him she would have come at least once, shown herself, so he would have seen her at least once, he could have gazed at her.... But she is stubborn—not once has she appeared.

Cold and frost hover over the mountains, yet Hryts continues riding his black steed from time to time, rushing off somewhere, then returning slowly in sadness. Only after the frosts began to bear down in earnest and heavy mounds of snow lay on the forest branches did he stop waiting for the girl in the forest. Melancholy settled in his soul, and no matter how the fair-faced Nastia tried to comfort him with her caresses, chatter and submissiveness, Hryts was no longer the way he used to be. He cannot send matchmakers to Tetiana because Nastia is a neighbour and he doesn't want to distress her. Added to this, his father won't give him any land, saying he must wait ... there's no rush to marry, he says, and he must abide by his father's wishes. While waiting thus and nursing God knows what hopes about Turkynia, he continues to make secret inquiries about her, to visit the blue-eyed Nastia at will, abandoning himself to the feelings that bind him to her and keep him there. He seems to gain an inner strength from hearing from his friends here and there that she sees no one in the village but him "who dances as though writing with his feet," that she is pining for him and loves him to distraction....

Turkynia is nowhere to be seen.

But Hryts is not one of those who remain discouraged for long. Early one morning he saddled his black-maned steed and rode to the village where Ivanykha Dub and her beautiful daughter lived. Riding about the village as if on private matters, he makes casual inquiries about Ivanykha Dub. Is she very proud and stand-offish—a very stern lady?

"Very proud," he is told, "and stern. As for her daughter, it seems that only a boyar will do."

"And the daughter?" he asks.

"Won't even listen about any suitor. So far she has rejected all of them," they tell him, "She says that none of them please her and will have nothing to do with them."

"She's a lively one, loving poor fellows," Hryts blurted out.

"What kind of 'loving' are you talking about? She accepts no one and as for a poor lad, she won't even look at him."

"Is she a beauty?" Hryts continues, pretending he does not know the girl.

"See for yourself," they reply. "Bow low to her, look at her brows, then judge with your own eyes who this Turkynia Dub is."

Hryts was warmed to the core. That is his Turkynia, the thought flashed through his mind. They are right, she looks at no one but him, she favours only him—that young and beautiful Turkynia Dub.

Only him? Ah, Hryts.... Be careful what you are doing!

"You think I'm ready to take anyone?" he recalls her words. "I'm not just for anyone...."

But Hryts is indifferent to these words. He loves her, and the young man lifts his head proudly as if demanding his right ... nothing else matters to him. Because "anyone" or not, she will be his! He has not met a girl yet who rejected him. Thinking thus, Hryts rides confidently to the home of Ivanykha Dub. At last he will see Tetiana, have a word or two with her. Maybe she will come out of the house....

* * *

Turkynia did come out, her face flushed, her brows lifted in amazement. Hryts stands before her, cap in hand.

"I have come, Turkynia," he says humbly.

"Good," she answered, her eyes smiling. Behind her came her mother, tall and stern and dressed in black.

"What is your business, young man?" she asked dryly, looking coldly from Hryts to her daughter.

"Has anyone been here this morning asking on my behalf?"

"No one," the answer was even colder.

"A man and a woman...."

"No one, I said!" and turning, went back into the house, saying: "And you come too daughter, don't stand outside!"

Thus Ivanykha Dub received him—and he saw her no more.

"I'm coming, Mother," says Tetiana obediently, without moving.

"Come and meet me, wherever you wish. I'll come anywhere, even to church," begs Hryts, bowing humbly again. "We'll sorrow a bit together, talk a bit."

"I won't come, Hryts, don't even wait," she answered resolutely.

He waits a moment, crumpling his cap in his hands, then says:

"Will you come into the woods in the spring?" bowing low to her, touching the ground with his cap.

"I'll come to the woods in the spring. Now you must go."

"When everything is green," continues Hryts, eagerly taking in her dark brows, her smiling lips, her beauty.

"When everything is green," she repeats, and smiles again.

Hryts bows.

"Thank you, Turkynia, for coming out of the house, for speaking to me—thank you again."

"Thank you for keeping your word, but you must go—Mother isn't joking."

Hryts practically flew on his black horse, and everything fell silent around the house, only the sound of horse's hooves floated back in the air, like a faint recollection.

"You'll come to the forest in the spring," Hryts repeats his question to himself at home, submerging himself in it wherever he goes, whatever he does.

"I'll come to the woods in the spring."

"When everything is green...."

"When everything is green...." Dear God, Turkynia does love him!

"Come, spring!" his young breast yearns mutely and prays, his heart sighs with passion, "Come, spring!..."

* * *

Hryts cheered up. In his secret happiness he embraces, caresses and fondles the blue-eyed Nastia. He pleases his father and mother, smiling to himself all the while. "You'll come to the woods in spring?" his heart asks.

"I'll come to the woods in spring."

"When everything is green?"

"When everything is green...."

Come, pines, grow green!

* * *

Spring arrived.

The firs stand like straight green banners, murmuring greetings and bowing their crests to each other. All because spring has come.

The flowers have also bloomed, blue-bells swing along the cliff-side among the rocks, and all in honour of spring, in honour of its return.

Young Tetiana's poppies have also budded and any moment now she will be able to pick them to adorn herself, then hurry on swift feet through the green forest to visit old Mavra, or even further....

                                    * * *

One such beautiful spring day Hryts went up into the mountain pastures to inspect the cattle and some of the shepherd's cottages, and at his father's request, to select some of the finer heads of cattle for sale.

Crossing the village toward the opposite mountain, where his father's pastures stretched, he met old Andronati, whom he has known since childhood, and who always, at least once every few years, appeared in their village and dropped by their house.

He visited for various reasons. Sometimes he came with spoons for sale, at other times simply for charitable offerings, and sometimes only to rest a while. But he always visited them. Now seeing the old gypsy on the empty road, Hryts greeted him warmly and stopped to talk.

The ancient gypsy joined the young man and slowly they exchanged news about how they were keeping, what had happened since the last time they had met, and all sorts of little details about their lives.

The old gypsy told Hryts that he had now been wandering the world for some twenty years and only stopped in Hungary on the open plains to spend the winter with some gypsies. His wife had died more than twenty years ago, shortly after losing their only daughter, who had met with misfortune and was either dead or also wandering the world. Their daughter's child, true, was doing very well, he said, without looking at the young man while saying this. The one thought that keeps him going is that one day he may close his eyes forever next to that child. Before that happens, though, he must wander the world. But when the time comes for his grandson to marry, he will come to him and stay.

During the past winter, he continued his tale, he passed through these neighbouring villages gathering alms, because the gypsies with whom he generally stayed had quarrelled among themselves and driven him out into the world alone to search for bread. But how can he earn anything when he can no longer pull a violin bow or spend whole evenings playing at weddings? He was suddenly seized with the desire to come through this village where he had last seen his daughter, but he regrets it now. He entered the forest by some path that he thought would bring him closer to the road and got lost. And though he had begged to be admitted to some little house in the forest, he didn't reach any warmth and nearly died of hunger and cold in the snow. Since then he spends the winter in the valleys. But he has become completely feeble, he feels that death is near. It seems to him, sometimes, that God has kept him standing so that in some way he can still render a service to his grandson.

"In what way?" asked Hryts.

The old man finds it difficult to explain this, but that is how it seems to him. Besides, he wants very much to live long enough to play his violin at his grandson's wedding, even with his old fingers. The old musician, Andronati, will play at his wedding ... afterwards ... he can die immediately. And that's that!

While recounting this, the old gypsy examined the young man, with searching eyes, seeing how vigourously he was dashing up the hill, like a stag. And so as not to leave the old man too far behind, Hryts would sit down from time to time and wait, indifferently watching the old man's slow progress and the old man himself.

"This is the third time I have seen you, my son," he explained to the young man, "it seems you have no parents."

"They say I don't," answered Hryts shortly, for he did not like being reminded that he was a foster-son.

"But you're doing very well? The old man asked with interest, and seemed to be waiting breathlessly to hear the word "well" on the young man's lips.

"Yes, well," he hears another short reply.

"You live with wealthy people?"

"You could say that. I have enough to eat and drink, they provide me with fine clothing, they gave me the finest horse in the village...," here he stopped without completing his thought.

"Then what is it that you're missing?" asks the old man laughing, "a sweetheart?"

Hryts waved his hand.

"There are enough of them," he says, "I can have my pick, and I've chosen two from among them."

"Are they rich?" the old man wants to know, and his eyes lit up greedily.

"Well, they seem to be. The dark one, they say, is rich, so maybe her mother won't allow her to marry me; the blue-eyed fair one is the one my parents want me to marry, and her parents, too. She is a good girl and pretty, exactly right for me, they say. But then God only knows which of them will be my fate. Whichever of them it will be, will be. So...," and he waved a hand nonchalantly, "they're all alike."

"What?" asks the old man, open-mouthed, for sometimes he does not hear very well.

"With all this going on, I'd like to go out into the world!" says Hryts.

"Where?" cried the old man.

"Into the world."

"Into the world? Like a gypsy? What a thing to say. To suffer, like me?"

"Oh no, not like you, begging for charity, but just like that, to see the world. I'm bored here among the hills. Yes, Grandpa, sometimes I have a hankering to go out somewhere into the world," says Hryts, almost yearningly.

"You're sorry for the girls, or what?" asked the old man, bursting into laughter.

"Maybe I am, especially for the one with the dark brows," Hryts answered simply. "She is never boring, always seems to feed you something new. To tell the truth, Grandpa, she's a beautiful girl."

"I'm telling you, son, what you're saying is all fiddle-faddle. Beautiful or not, fair or dark—if she's rich, take her! If she's too beautiful, then beware. She'll soon have her eye on others," the old man warns.

Hryts burst out laughing.

"And what about me?" he asked. "But she is beautiful, like a boyar's daughter. Yet the fair one is affectionate and tries to please. Whatever I want, she's ready to do it. The boys would give their eye teeth for either of them. I still don't know which one I'll marry. I hate to give up one, and I would be sorry to leave the other. Hey, Turkynia, Turkynia!" suddenly he cried out sadly, "you've crept into my heart, and like a sorceress, have hidden yourself well! Come on girls, why don't you blend into one and then I'll marry the both of you!"

At these sad and impassioned words the old man laughed harshly. Like some ancient fairytale, he recalled the unhappy love affair of his daughter, Mavra. She had loved her husband Radu, and the Hungarian boyar, too—then she was left alone ... disappearing somewhere into the world....

"Love only one, son...," he warns him gravely. "Love only one, and faithfully."

He stopped, as though afraid to explain his words, to complete his thought, to say what his tongue wants to say. He is silent, reluctant to drive away this beloved boy and alienate him forever.

"I'll probably marry the fair one," Hryts spoke up at last, "No matter that I may love the dark one best. But where is she? Who could hold her? She is here ... and there ... here and there, and when you want to embrace her, hold her close, she is 'not for you.' God only knows how everything will turn out. The parents are all for the fair one, only I know the dark one. We love each other in secret, meeting in the forest.... Turkynia, come out!" he cried sadly, ignoring the presence of the old gypsy, as if he were all alone in the mountains. "She'll come when everything is green!... But everything is green already," he added, turning to the old man as though he were seeing him for the first time, "and you ... Oh-h!" again he cried from the depths of his heart. Then throwing down his hat, he hurled himself down on the grass.

The old man crept to him, then stopped to rest.

"You and the dark-browed one are secretly in love?" he asked.

"We always meet in the forest. The mother won't receive me in their house yet, guarding her like a she-wolf, she doesn't even want to talk. So we meet secretly in the forest."

"That is wrong, my boy," the old man warns again, then he sank into deep thought. "Wrong, be careful. The world is full of curses, someone may curse you out of grief for her."

"But she is so beautiful!" Hryts explains, paying no attention to the old man's words, but, rising quickly to his feet with a capricious gesture, adjusts his hat at a rakish angle. "All the boys are after her, but I, Grandad," he adds proudly and sincerely, as if he were satisfying something in himself by submitting to his desire to speak, "I alone will have her. She is beautiful, I say, and like a wild goat she darts through the forest, that's where we love one another."

"And I, my son, advise you to love only one," the old man spoke up again, leaning on his cane in front of him, "only one, and love her faithfully. Don't caress two. It leads to sin, no matter how a man may protect himself." He sighed deeply and sadly, then asked suddenly: "What is her name? Could she be a gypsy if she's dark?"

Hryts howled.

"What a guess!" he cried. "You crawled out of a tent yourself and you would push another into it...." And again he laughed.

"Don't mock the gypsies!" warned the old man in a rather malicious tone, "because you yourself do not know where you come from. Just think—you are drawn to the world in spite of having plenty of bread and salt. And what will happen next, you do not know yet. It's true your face is white, but who was your mother, who was your father? A gypsy or a boyar—you don't know."

The boy flew into a rage.

"Silence, gypsy!" he cried, "and don't say another word. If I get really angry, I'll throw you over the cliff before you even realize it. Imagine," he added arrogantly, "he reminds me of my mother. Hear, hear!" and in his rage he whistled. But he quickly calmed down. "My dark-browed love is Turkynia, Grandad," he added. "Do you know her? Have you heard of her? You're like a sleep-walker, dragging yourself around the world," and be began to laugh again.

"I do not know her, but if you wish, I'll find out … and maybe I'll be able to help you someday. But I don't know her."

"Of course not.… As if she would be consorting with gypsies," Hryts jabbed at the old man arrogantly.

"No," says the old man meekly, "just loving one."

Hryts did not understand, and fell silent. He felt confused by the gypsy's reply. Neither comprehending, nor wanting to ask, but for some reason he became grave.

"If I only knew when you will be getting married, I would drag myself there," the old man spoke up even more meekly. "Even from far, far away, son," he said humbly, bowing almost to the ground, "even from far, far away … I'd just watch and look until I've had enough of it. But it's not for me, son, an old man and a poor old man at that, to watch a wedding between two wealthy young people."

"I'll get married in the fall," Hryts interrupted him proudly, "this very fall," as if to himself. "Come, if you like. We show kindness to the poor here, so why not to an old gypsy? Come with your fiddle.…"

The old man bowed again, meekly:

"Yes, I would like to come."

Hryts stood before him, young and handsome, and gazed over the old man's head far into the distance, over the forest and mountains, as if expecting someone.

"What are you looking for? What are you thinking about?"

Hryts shrugged.

"About the dark-browed one, Grandpa…," he admitted. "She has me so tied up in knots that I can't stop thinking about her, and who knows if she'll be mine?"

"If I were a seer, I'd tell your fortune, even here on the hillside," answered the old man, holding the boy back so he could look his fill. "If not, then maybe I can be of use to you in some other way … between the girls, so you won't be so troubled about them."

"You don't say!" Hryts objected, "I'm not afraid of them. I'll do as I please."

"Then I guess I'll just play at your wedding before I die...."

"At the wedding," repeated Hryts with a forced smile.

"God willing. *I will play one last time only for you.* I would like to see you become the wealthiest man in the village. I have known you since childhood and your parents have always been kindness itself to me. That's why I'd be happy to ... even though I'm a poor man ... and a gypsy stranger ... I'd be happy to," suddenly he bowed his grey head to his chest and was silent.

"Maybe one day I will be rich," said Hryts, "I don't know. They say that the dark-browed girl's wealth has no equal in the village, so who knows if she'll be allowed to marry me."

The old man was astonished.

"In which way is she the richest?"

Hryts stared at him and in a minute burst out laughing. "In which way? With her dark brows."

"Ah, like an enchantress?"

"A real enchantress, Grandpa."

"Be careful, son. Dark brows have great power."

"They say they do," answers Hryts, laughing again. "But I'm not afraid of her. If only her mother will allow her to marry me."

"One has to use all one's strength and vigour against enchantresses," the old man explains in all seriousness, "or else they begin to control a man. We gypsies are always on guard against them."

"I'm not afraid of them, and I'll do as I please. No girl is the equal of Hryts.... And then, I also have the fair one.... I won't give in to either of them. They will ... to me," and with these words Hryts smoothed his moustache, smiling and drawing himself up with dignity.

Just as twenty years earlier Andronati had stood with his white grandchild in his arms on the hilltop, looking down on the village spread out below to find the home of a wealthy family, now it seemed that Hryts was also looking in vain over the forest and mountains, as if seeking his fate that was to arrive from one of the girls.

At that moment the melancholy and protracted sound of a trembita rose from somewhere in the hills, as it had twenty years earlier.

Hryts paused.

"Is this for death?" asked the old man.

"I don't know. Maybe," answered the boy, walking with great haste.

Although he was accustomed to the sound of the trembita, and loved it, he reacted painfully to the sound.

The old man, unable to keep up with him, stopped to catch his breath.

Hryts also paused for a moment.

"I'll leave you now, son, and return to the valley. I don't have the strength to go any further."

"Go ahead," answered Hryts. "I'm in a hurry because they're waiting for me at the pasture."

"Go on then, son, go with God," said the old man. "I'm glad to have seen you, and may God's will take care of the future."

"You'll see me again at the wedding," Hryts consoled him kindly, and suddenly, as if responding to some internal command, he lifted his hat humbly and bowed low to Andronati.

"Grandfather, bless me before the wedding," he asked. "Who knows what may happen, for you might not be able to come. Bless me now, for you are an old man."

Old Andronati was shaken with emotion and began weeping.

"Bless you, my son," his voice trembled. "I wish you all that is good and happy—and don't forget your grandfather...."

"I won't forget, Father."

Hryts went on his way, and his heart seemed to be filled with a kind of yearning or palpitations of happiness, overlaid with thoughts of his wedding. At length he paused and looked down the path, where the old man who called himself his grandfather was standing.

There he was.

The old man turned and began walking down the path further into the valley until he disappeared from view.

* * *

The surrounding mountains stand riveted; the dense forest stands motionless. Only the hawks, their wings outstretched, hover luxuriously over them beneath the blue canopy of the sky.

* * *

Early spring has already passed; the forest and the mountains are flaunting their brightest verdure—summer is on its way.

For the fourth Sunday in a row now Hryts has mounted his black horse to ride into the forest to seek Turkynia, but she does not come. He always sets out with high hopes and returns dejected. Maybe she has already been betrothed during the carnival period before Lent, he sometimes thinks anxiously, or maybe her mother has sent her away somewhere and he has heard nothing about it—no one is saying anything.

He sank into a deep melancholy. If no one else notices it, his black horse certainly does. While waiting impatiently in the forest, Hryts sometimes stands for hours, leaning against him deep in thought, or singing a melancholy tune, or once again listening for the rustle that might be announcing her presence in the forest, or playing his flute. In the end, discouraged, he mounts the horse and drives him hard in any direction for consolation, or back to the talkative, obedient, blue-eyed Nastia, who comforts him, as always. So it is today.

Leaning against his black-maned friend, Hryts gazes with a sharp, hawk-like eye up the White Path stretching down from the mountain and out of the thick green forest toward him.

"Will she come?" he hopes.

No way to tell.

The sun is sinking lower as the afternoon advances, but she does not appear.

He had counted all the hawks that had floated in the clear air above, with his eyes had measured the length and breadth of the dark gorge through which the river rushed boisterously, filling it with his longing thoughts, and she had not come today either.

"Will you come to the forest in the spring?" he had asked her in the winter.

"I'll come to the forest in the spring."

"When everything turns green?"

"When everything turns green," she had answered smiling and this is how she kept her word! Not only had she not come, she had not once appeared anywhere this summer. How was one to believe girls? Not like his Nastia: she knew his wishes before he even articulated them—she was able to read his thoughts. That was the Nastia that he was fond of. She was honest and sincere with him, truly sincere. But Turkynia?

Hryts grits his teeth impatiently and curses her as a "she-devil" who made a fool of him that day last winter by making an empty promise for the springtime, which she never intended to keep.

While Hryts is thinking these unhappy thoughts, his horse suddenly raises his head high, his glittering black eyes looking immovably in one direction of the forest, his ears pricked up as if he is waiting, almost as if his entire body is waiting....

The wide-winged branches of the firs near them suddenly part without a rustle and a girl's head adorned with large red poppies appears between them, then disappears again. The horse gives a start, but Hryts, deep in thought, does not notice what has startled his friend, and throws himself at him. What has frightened the horse, surprised him? Has he seen a bear? Or perhaps a long-legged doe that wanted to cross the White Path, was startled at the sight of him and hid. He calmed the frightened animal and the earlier silence descended around them again. Nothing moves. They wait.

Is there really nothing moving?

Nothing.

On the contrary, there is some movement. The horse stood quietly for a while, immobile, then begins to move uneasily. Sensing something unfamiliar, he began to gaze about, his head raised high, but showing less fear than he did earlier. Hryts tied him to a fir, then started up the White Path. He had gone no more than a few steps when the branches of a fir alongside the path parted like before to make way for a girl's splendidly-adorned head, then reveal the entire tall and slender figure of Tetiana.

"Turkynia, it's you!" cried Hryts delightedly.

"It is I."

It is I! It is *she*!

And neither of them know exactly how it happened that he is holding her in his embrace, their lips meeting in a kiss.

"Let me go!" at last she demands sternly, and frees herself, alarmed by his embrace, as if his arms, forgetting how to move, will imprison her forever.

"Turkynia!" he repeats, besides himself with happiness, "I've waited here for you so many times, yearned for you so often, and you never appeared until today."

"Until today," she repeats, laughing, then adds, "so let me go." She frees herself impatiently.

"I didn't come alone," she quickly explains, "I'm with another woman" (she could never overcome her desire to mention Mavra). "... Quiet," she whispers, "she comes this way sometimes to the White Rock, looking for herbs...."

"As long as she doesn't come here!" he interrupts, embracing her again. "Let her not come here, or I'll throw her into the ravine straight away. Today is Sunday, and you've come at last.... I have not waited in vain, my star, so let's hope she won't come."

Looking up at him, her dark brows raised in amusement, she asks:

"You say that you waited here for me many times?"

"Today is the fourth Sunday I've waited."

"And I've walked the forest, but always turned back, somehow I couldn't continue toward you...."

He gazes into her eyes that have never seen evil, that always look directly and simply, wonderingly, trustingly....

"My cuckoo!" he says tenderly, holding her close, kissing her, "My cuckoo."

"I couldn't, I just couldn't," she continues to assure him, "I deceived my mother, I didn't tell her I was going into the forest, my conscience always stopped me."

"From loving, Turkynia?"

"From loving, Hryts."

"But you see, I can."

"Love and deceive?"

"Deceive and love!" he answers without thinking and laughs.

"And I'm always hesitating."

"Because you don't love as deeply as I do."

"Hryts!"

"Turkynia!..."

She clasps her arms around his neck and is silent.

"Turkynia.... Do you love me truly?"

Silence.

Then: "Maybe, Hryts...."

"My cuckoo!"

She lifts her head and again looks into his eyes, directly and candidly:

"Never ask me that way again," she begs urgently.

"But you are always so strange with me," he apologizes.

"No, Hryts, no...," she assures him and presses against him trustingly and fervently, "If you only knew...."

"What, my girl?"

"How difficult it is to love deeply and at the same time hide that love...," she pauses for a moment, then continues guiltily, "from your mother."

"Why hide it," he asks simply. "Is it shameful to love?"

"She wouldn't let me go into the forest," she explains, "She'd ask why you don't send matchmakers and wouldn't allow me to meet you. Oh, no... My mother would never allow it."

"My-my!" he comforts her, laughing.

"Yes, yes, Hryts," she repeats gravely. "There's no joking with my mother. She's very strict where boys are concerned, she doesn't trust them."

"In spite of which you can't even ride around them on a horse." He laughed again.

"It's easy for you to laugh," she says, looking him in the eyes, waiting.

"It's easy," he answers cheerfully, "why shouldn't it be when Turkynia is beside me? When the time is right there will also be matchmakers. They will definitely come this fall. This past winter was so long and so difficult. I longed for you so much that now, in the middle of glorious summer, I should start being afraid of mothers? Don't be afraid of anything with me."

Saying this, he takes her in his arms again with unrestrained passion.

"You love me very much?" she asks, trying to fathom the depth of his love for her by his eyes—eyes to which she has lost her heart.

"I have never loved anyone the way I love you. I've already told you—only you in the whole world. If you only knew, Turkynia...."

"And if you only knew," she interrupts gravely, arching her dark eyebrows, and somehow expressing more with them than with her words.

"You have no idea what is in my heart," he assures her, once again drawing her into his arms.

"And I, Hryts.... And I—Oh God!" she did not finish her sentence.

"Love me, my cuckoo, love me!" he implores, "and I'll carry you to your home in my arms."

Suddenly she raises her poppy-adorned head, as if returning for a moment from another world, and asks with extraordinary gravity:

"And when you have stopped loving me?"

"Turkynia, my star ... as if I could? Why are you asking so sadly?"

"Because you may even part from me with a whistle, when you have stopped loving me," she answered. "But I, Hryts ... but I...," she stops and seeks refuge against his chest, "I...." Her words trailed off, she fell silent as if she had given away her soul.

"I have whistled, Turkynia," he explains seriously, "I have, truly, and at more than one. But I fell in love with you so wholeheartedly, that sooner you will trifle with my feelings, if a wealthier suitor comes along, than I with yours. Am I not right, Tetiana? Ivanykha Dub is known far and wide as a wealthy woman, and I am just Hryts. My only wealth is my horse and my loving heart," and saying this he kissed her and drew her to him with such sincere passion that it silenced her.

"Sometimes during the winter," she began after a moment, "before you came and stood before our house, I went about with such heaviness in my heart and prayed God to turn you away from me, then you came and stood before me. Hryts," she added, putting her arms around his neck, "from that time on, I couldn't forget you."

"It was my longing for you that drove me to your home," he explained merrily. "I couldn't wait any longer, so I saddled my horse and flew to you. Whatever will be, will be, I thought. At least I will see her, at least see those dark brows, look into the eyes that have stolen my heart, have sunk into my soul, taken away my peace of mind and then hidden from me."

"Mother asked questions about you later," she began again, "who you were, how did I get to know you. When I didn't say, she stopped, only warning: 'Be careful, Tetiana!' I'm afraid of my mother, Hryts, when she is silent, but still, I couldn't forget you. I saw you in my dreams on your horse, I yearned for you in my dreams. During the day I hid my feelings by keeping busy, and on sleepless nights, I fed on memories. I couldn't do anything else. That's how I lived through the winter."

"I would have come to visit you at least once or twice more, Turkynia," said Hryts, "but your haughty mother turned me away, but don't forget me now. Don't forget to love me, and you'll see that in time everything will turn out as we wish."

"I did not forget. Haven't I come?" she arches her eyebrows questioningly.

"Thank you, lass, my beautiful flower, just love me faithfully and wait until fall."

"And you?" she asks, her whole soul smiling into his beautiful eyes, "Will you come? You won't forget? You won't fall in love with someone else?"

He takes her in his arms.

"I love only you, only you in the whole world. I'll come again on Sunday, I'll wait for you. Come here through the forest, blossom in it like a flower. I'll be here."

"Always through the forest?" she asks, pondering, not certain whether to agree....

"Always through the forest."

"Maybe not," she suddenly speaks up and pushes him away, turning briskly.

"Turkynia!"

She is not listening and continues to walk.

"Turkynia! Are you rushing off to your mother?"

"Yes."

"Oh, well!"

She walks on, silent.

He rushed after her.

"Tetiana," he pleads. "See, you're angry again. Have you already stopped loving me? And I've waited so long ... shoot me, so I won't yearn for you any more.... It will be easier for you...."

She looked back and stopped, silently drawing her brows into a frown.

He devours her with his eyes, then draws her silently to him in farewell. Silently, she presses against him, sinking into his love without protest.

"You'll come again?" he whispers passionately, pleadingly, putting heart and soul into the question.

"I'll come."

"Remember!"

*   *   *

When at last he returned to his horse, he could not resist asking her one more time:

"Do you love me?" His voice pursued her questioningly through the thick forest, and waited.

From among the slender high firs, sounding at first as if from the opposite mountain across the ravine, came a clear echo: "Love me?"

"Love yo-oo-u!" a young voice called out strongly, and flying into the depths of the forest, it paused for a moment. Then, like a young wanderer, it fought its way through the forest to his ears: "Love yo-oo-u...," and having reached him, disappeared for all time.

*   *   *

And so Tetiana walks the forest every Sunday. She flies up the hill lightly, with bliss in her eyes, so he will not have to wait long ... then runs down again so as not to be late, not to anger her mother, keeping these meetings a secret.... And always hurrying.

Week passes after week, like a single day, summer blooms luxuriantly while their love grows stronger....

"Come, my Turkynia, don't begrudge your love...," he begs her sincerely every time they met, and as long as the White Path winds its way alongside the forest, he walks along it with her. He always grieves to leave her ... he loves her so much ... she is so beautiful.

"You'd better go back," she sometimes reminds him, standing in his way, so he will not go further.

"You begrudge me another minute?" he reproaches her, "my only happiness is you, more than anything else in the whole world, and this is what you're like," he adds bitterly.

"I, Hryts? I?" she asks in wonder, her eyes mirroring her hurt.

"You. You don't love as I do, you're always hesitating, always as if at a crossroad, or as if running on hot coals."

"Hryts!" she protests, then falls silent. Quick and sensitive, after a minute she makes an effort to reply, even though she is offended:

"I've submerged myself in you, I know no others, I deceive my mother ... and you...." She does not finish.

"You are still wavering, Turkynia."

"I am hesitating because I'm not sure if you truly love me. Oh, Hryts," she entreats, looking at him with large eyes, "don't deceive me. I know my own heart, it is no longer in my bosom—it is yours. The thoughts I had about you earlier have changed. The soul that once was mine is now dragging itself after you. It will never again return to the past. Don't toy with me."

"But still you waver, Turkynia...."

Her eyes blazed.

"You tell me I don't love you truly? Oh-h-h!" she cried in despair, and with that pushed him away from her, like she did her mother when she was a child, when she wouldn't let her have her own way.

"By the time the snow falls you will be in my house," he says, instead of answering her, pulling her back into his arms to console her. "Don't regret loving," he implores, "my one happiness is that there is someone like you in the world. Always come, darling, don't forget me. And if you are scolded for wandering the forest, tell everyone to their face that you are seeking happiness."

"How, Hryts?" she asks, wondering.

"That you are looking for the fern blossom," he explains. "Don't you know? It brings happiness."

"I didn't know," she answers, surprised again by his quick inventiveness.

"The blossom of the fern," he explains further, "has to be searched for a long, long, time, but whoever finds it will then know everything there is to know in the world, and will find happiness. So say that. Who would forbid you to hunt this blossom? Your mother, perhaps? Come on, laugh!"

"Maybe ... my ... mother," she answers thoughtfully and falls silent.

"And before the snow falls," he repeats, "you'll be in my house."

"Before the snow falls," she repeats dreamily and as though another thought has struck her, adds fearfully: "I'm afraid, Hryts, it's so long to wait."

"Why are you afraid, dear heart?" he asks. "As long as you're with me, don't be afraid of anything. I love only you—only you will be mine. Don't worry about anything else!"

"Matchmakers are already being arranged for this fall," she complains and, seeking advice, embraces him.

"Matchmakers from whom?" he asks angrily.

"I wasn't told from whom, but Mother has hinted at it, she probably wants to get me married this year."

"Let her hint. I am first in line for you, so turn away all the others."

"I've already turned them away," she answers. "I know only you, but if I am forced, I'll tell Mother the truth. You are the son of wealthy parents, Mother will allow me to marry you."

"Your mother will let me marry you ... although," he says uncertainly....

"Although you love another?" she asks with failing heart.

Horrified, he answered quickly:

"No, not another, no Tetiana, but.... In truth, I...."

"What, Hryts?" she interrupts him with frightened eyes.

"I," then he breathed more easily, "To tell the truth, I'm not a rich man's son, but a poor orphan. I'm adopted—a foundling...."

"A foundling? How is that?"

"A foundling child, adopted. They are not my real parents."

"But Hryts," as if defending something, "you told me yourself that your father is rich.... Oh.... Don't...," and she stopped.

"I said it and I'm saying it again: my father is rich and maybe he'll leave me his property some day. He has no children of his own, only me. If you marry me he'll probably give me a goodly share ... and sometime in the future, maybe everything. I'm the only one they have, I call him father. In the meantime I'm poor—I have only you. Love me even though I'm poor! Don't desert me, Tetiana!"

"Hryts!" she responds with heartfelt sincerity, "I'll convince my mother. Even though she is strict, she loves me. You hear, Hryts, she loves me—she'll let us have our way. She won't separate us...."

"That's fine, my cuckoo," he is calmer, then adds: "But don't say anything yet, come to the forest, and before the snow falls, you'll be in my house."

Tetiana listens, then stepping closer, she gazes deeply, with wide open eyes, into his beautiful blue ones:

"Hryts, I love you," she says, "like no one else in the world. You know that, but...." She arched her brows, as though commanding something.

"Don't worry about anything, my Turkynia," he answers, ignoring the expression on her face, simply looking at her fondly, "Don't worry about anything. You are mine!"

"Yours," she repeats, and quickly taking the poppies out of her hair, she throws them at his feet. "Here, take them," she says, "and now go. I'm already very late. The sun is past the mountain now, it's setting, shooting its beams across the sky—Mother will scold me again for wandering about idly."

"Don't be afraid," he says, "I'm going." He embraces her for the last time. "You'll come again?" he asks, as he does every time, and their eyes meet in a single flame that only love can produce. "Come, my flower, call to me from the forest."

"I'll call again from the forest."

"Only the forest and I know Turkynia."

"And my mother, Hryts?" she asks abruptly, "God will not bless us for deceiving her. She is good, and she loves me ... and I...," she stops, shakes her head and moves away. But taking a few steps, she pauses for a moment and cries out in a low voice:

"Hryts!... Hryts!..."

He rushes to her side.

"Hryts!" she repeats, her lips distorted with bitterness.

"What is it?" he asks, smiling tenderly with his blue eyes, "Forgot to say that you love me again? Then tell me once more, I'm listening...."

"When will we see each other again, Hryts?" she asked, her brows raised in question.

"I don't know yet, but we will.... You'll come?"

"I'll come," and with these words, she turned and disappeared into the forest. The branches closed behind her, shaking slightly.

Hryts does not leave immediately. He fusses around his horse, picks up the red poppies, his heart filled with wonder.

"I've got you, Turkynia," the thought fills his being, "I've got you!"

"I'll come," he repeats to himself, and begins to reflect on her words. It was odd the way she said them: "I'll come...," then she had gone away from him sadly.

He comes to with a start, listening.... It sounded as though her voice were coming from the right side of the forest. He strains to hear, waiting, and all around everything also seems to be listening ... and waiting.

"Don't forget!" her voice breaks through to him.

"Don't forget!" An echo through the forest demands and dies away.

"Don't forget!" the words break through to him.

Hryts does not answer. Instead he mounted his horse and rode away.

* * *

"Mavra!"

"What is it, daughter? You've come to see old Mavra at last? With your love affair, you've forgotten that she exists?"

Tetiana hugs her old nanny warmly, then snuggles up to her and entreats her:

"Forgive me, Mavra, for not coming to see you. It just wasn't possible for me to come. There's been a lot to do at home, and Sunday...."

"And Sunday?" asks the gypsy, her dark eyes glittering in challenge at the young girl before her. "And Sunday?"

"Like Sunday, Mavra!" answers Tetiana, and turns away from the old woman.

But in a minute her good mood is restored.

"Mavra," she admits, "you know that I love Hryts."

"Yes, you told me, child," answers the gypsy, still looking closely at the girl, "you told me."

"And he loves me."

"And as sincerely as you love him?"

"Mavra!" cries the girl reproachfully, and turns away wounded by the old woman, who remains calm. "I'll never tell you anything again. You either don't believe me, or make fun of me. No matter what I tell you, you never believe me. Shame on you, Mavra...."

"God be with you, child!" Mavra says in a soothing, humble manner, "I have never seen him, let alone...."

"Haven't seen, haven't seen!" Tetiana repeats angrily. "And disbelief and hatred is always in your voice. You never believe. I know. You don't believe the whole world any more. I remember very well what you told me about yourself, what you lived through because of deception—but, Mavra, I trust him alone in the whole world. He loves me truly, Mavra. Oh! You don't understand!"

"Child, I believe that he loves you," answers Mavra firmly. "Who would not love you, my lovely star and good as an angel? Whom should one love in this world if not those like you? Ha-i, ha-i!" she sang out suddenly, swaying back and forth, "ha-i, ha-i!"

Tetiana was appeased.

"Before the snow falls, he said, Mavra, I'll be in his house."

"Glory be to God!" answers Mavra in a more conciliatory tone, and sighs with relief. "You must hurry, because when autumn comes your mother will be receiving other matchmakers. She told me recently that she wants to see you married this fall, then she'll enter a nunnery."

"Oh, Mother goes on and on about this!" says Tetiana. "What she wants most in life is to go into a nunnery in her old age."

"Perhaps it's a good thing, child."

"But for whom will she be doing so much praying? She prays enough as it is ... every Sunday, holidays...."

"Perhaps for your happiness," answers the old woman, "you are all she has. Ever since your father died, with whom she lived so well, as she and other people say, she has been drawn to the nunnery. Who else would pray for your happiness, child, if not your mother? You know, she would bring the very heavens to you if she could."

"That's true," concedes Tetiana thoughtfully, then adds: "She is one, and you, Mavra, are the second, and he the third, who love me sincerely and truly."

"You are quite right, child. For a woman a good husband is the same as a father and mother."

"Isn't that the truth, Mavra," says Tetiana, her eyes shining with inner happiness.

"True. If only you would let me see him at least once, child," she suggested "Don't hide him like a golden sovereign any more."

Tetiana smiled gaily:

"You'll see him, Mavra, you'll see him, so handsome, Mavra, that ... O-o-oh!"

"Like you?"

"He is tall, with a black moustache, but fair and blue-eyed. He always rides a coal-black horse. Then he is really at his best. He rides him like the wind. Oh, Mavra—he is so handsome!"

Mavra listens, her thoughts flitting somewhere into the past.

"That's what *he* was like," she says finally, more to herself than to Tetiana, "Tall as an oak, as the saying goes, fair of face, blue-eyed, flying like the wind on his horse past our tents on the Hungarian plain. That's what he was like, And always whistling. He was a lord, Tetiana."

"Who are you talking about, Mavra?" asks the girl whose thoughts at this moment are full of Hryts.

putting it together

) "About the one, child, for whom I squandered my destiny, lost my father and mother, my husband Radu, and in the end, my child. The one because of whom I am now all alone on this whole mountain, this whole forest, the entire world. If only they had left me my child," she said sorrowfully, "the world would have been a good place for me, instead of what I have.... Oh Radu, Radu!..." she cried bitterly, "was there no other punishment you could have given me but banishment from the clan? Better to have killed me on the spot, as you promised. Better to have left me, gone away by yourself, and Father and Mother would have taken me back, but now...." And she went on complaining as she always did when she talked about this, her body swaying in the gypsy fashion, her voice almost a sing-song in her sorrow and bitterness.

"Quiet, Mavra, quiet," Tetiana soothes her. "Don't grieve so much. It won't help you now in any way. Maybe the child is with God, waiting for you, one day he will greet you, and maybe it is better so."

"Greet me?" asks Mavra sorrowfully, then regaining her composure, begins in a different tone of voice; "He would now be a young man somewhere, perhaps in service, earning his keep for himself and his mother, and it would be fine for him and his mother. But now what? Ha-i, ha-i!" she wailed again, "ha-i, ha-i!"

"Maybe he is earning somewhere, Mavra, who knows," says Tetiana calmly. "So God has willed. In truth, Mavra, you betrayed your husband Radu, and that's how this whole tragedy began."

"Betrayed because I was young, foolish and trusting," answers Mavra, now calm. "I was so taken with the fair, noble face, his un-gypsy-like eyes, rich attire, that God punished me. Stay with your own, he says, and punishes. Be it bad, or good, but it won't end in sin."

The girl listened silently, as though gazing into the distance, though there were only the low walls of the old house before her and nothing else.

"Hryts is not wealthy," she says finally, saying the name of her love confidently and firmly. "Hryts is not wealthy, but he is fair and blue-eyed, and rides a horse like the wind. And we love each other." Saying this, she rises to bid Mavra farewell. "Come see us, Mavra, if sometimes I don't come to see you on a Sunday."

"Ha-i, ha-i!" answers Mavra. "I'll come. And if you can't come on a Sunday, then come during the week and tell an old woman when she should prepare for a wedding and see your young man."

"Soon, Mavra, soon," answers Tetiana, and leaves.

"And don't go out to meet him in the forest every Sunday," cautions

Mavra, following the girl out of the house, "and when you do, take me with you," she jokes with an odd look. "Let him take a look at his beloved's old nanny. After all, it was she who brought her up like a star for his happiness; fed her on folktales, caressed with her heart, guarded with her eyes. So let him at least thank her now with a kindly word."

"He'll thank you, Mavra, he will!" answers Tetiana with dignity. "He is good and kind and you'll be convinced for yourself that he loves me truly, if you don't believe me."

A few steps from the house Tetiana suddenly looks back. Was it just her imagination or had Mavra chuckled to herself when she turned away? Had she really done that?

No.

At that moment Mavra was stepping over the threshold of her house, as though she had disappeared into a pit.

No, she must have imagined it.

Tetiana, feeling humiliated and abased, as if she has been doused with cold water, walks home dejectedly.

She had resolved so many times not to tell Mavra anything about Hryts, about her love, and always her love and trust in her old nanny overcome her scruples; she betrays herself and talks.

Then she goes home again, like today, with venom in her soul, an aching heart and the grief of mistrust in him until she sees him again, until with his bright, sky-blue eyes he eases her saddened heart again with his explanations, soothes her into trusting once again.

"Hryts!" yearns her warm, open heart, throbbing with its pure, undivided love, "Hryts, is it so? You love me?"

"Ha-i, ha-i!" Again she seems to hear the warning voice of the old gypsy, sounding as though it is driving away some bird of prey, and her soul is pierced through with a sharp pang of grief. "Ha-i, ha-i!"

Tetiana burst into tears.

* * *

Returning home, Tetiana kneels silently in the quiet room before the icon of the Blessed Virgin Mary and wrings her hands, as she did a year ago, pressing them to her breast and her brow in desperation, repeating the same phrase over and over again:

"Lord, why am I sad? Why am I sad? I am miserable, oh Lord!..."

* * *

Several years ago, a grey-haired wanderer, who was resting a few days at the home of the pious and compassionate Ivanykha Dub, told a group of Tetiana's young friends who had gathered there, that there used to be a custom that may still exist, according to which Ukrainian girls tell fortunes on St. John's Eve[5] and try to find out from the water nymphs what the future holds in store for them.

"How? With what?" the girls asked the old man with interest.

He does not know exactly, he is not from that area, but he remembers some of it and he will tell them. Late at night on St. John's Eve, he explains, the girls sail in boats on the river, or, if they are afraid that the water nymphs will lure them into the river depths and turn them into nymphs, they walk along the shore singing various melancholy love songs, beautiful and enticing. The girls are splendidly dressed, their heads adorned with wreaths of flowers, and singing in chorus on the boats or on the shore, they remove the wreaths from their heads and throw them into the water. After throwing them into the water they wait, singing and watching to see where the water carries their wreaths, or if they will be thrown up on shore, if such is their destiny. Sometimes the water-nymphs like to scatter the wreaths about in the water—this is a sign that girls have a disloyal nature and will not hold onto their loved one. Occasionally, a wreath thrown into the water sinks—this is a sign that either the girl or her loved one will die within a year, or else part. Sometimes the wreath is held on the side of the stream from which the loved one will appear. But always the wreaths are summoned and lured by the nymphs using their power and strength, out of gratitude that the young girls remember them on St. John's Eve, dress up in their honour and with youthful charming songs revive them, who are bound by a magic spell to the waters. They reciprocate by predicting their destiny, revealing it to the girls through various occurrences understood only by the girls, or through wonderful dreams that reveal their future.

And the girls were fascinated by the tale that was recounted by the old wanderer.

In spite of their interest, however, they did not hurry to carry out this

---

5. This day is known as "Ivana Kupala" in Ukrainian, Kupalo being the pagan god of love.

fortune-telling. Some did not want to because there were no boats, others refused, explaining that they were afraid that the nymphs might entice them into joining them in the water, others hesitated because the young men would find out and laugh at them. This went on until finally not one was willing to try.

That is how it was a few years ago.

But this year things turned out differently.

This year, God only knows why, Tetiana had the notion to find out what fate had in store for her. Her young friends, to whom she revealed her desire to tell fortunes on St. John's Eve with wreaths, seemed to have been awaiting just such an invitation, an invitation from the most beautiful, and in their opinion, the most courageous girl among them, who always assured them that she was afraid of nothing—neither of the nymphs by day or night, nor of the derision of all the boys in the village; she just wanted to do it. She wanted to see where her wreath will float, in what direction the nymphs will take it. Therefore she invited her friends to a St. John's Eve festival by the stream, a little distance from the mill.

The girls accepted her invitation eagerly; suddenly they, too, were seized with an enthusiastic desire to tell their fortunes with their wreaths, enjoy an evening along the river bank, sing the most popular songs, and win the favour of the nymphs hidden at the bottom of the stream.

The long-awaited evening arrived at last and with it a full moon.

Tomorrow was St. John the Baptist's Day and tonight was bright and starlit, as if it had blossomed on purpose to allow the girls to learn their future fate and who their loved one will be.

Like beautiful birds they gathered on the banks of the river which, illuminated by the full moon, sparkled enticingly between the heavily-forested, night-darkened Chabanytsia Mountain and the White Path that ran alongside.

Like a broad silver stream, the murmuring waters of the river moved forward, ever forward.

But it was not the same everywhere.

In the place where the river narrowed for a moment, and where a mighty boulder has lifted its immovable form, the river becomes more stately. There, under the boulder, which resembles a small cliff, it safeguards, like secrets, a number of pockets of turbulent depths, over which its surface wrinkles, eddies and whirls.

Wrinkling and shuddering with some kind of gloatingly malicious and beguiling scintillation, it tries mercilessly to swallow everything that appears on its surface.

No one has ever ventured to cross these depths, so treacherous are they in their surface tranquillity. No one has even tried to swim across them.

They are not interesting.

They attract no one with their tranquillity, and whoever is lured there for a moment turns away, realizing the hidden depths surrounding the mighty boulder. At this point the river itself is seemingly deserted, and no one disturbs its serenity.

* * *

The girls were not alone in their planned adventure on the banks of the sparkling moonlit stream. Among them is the gypsy, Mavra. Attired in some ancient red kerchief that is sliding carelessly off her head, her hair dishevelled, with an old silver necklace that is hanging from her neck, she stalks among the girls like a phantom.

Exhilarated by the girlish babble and the gifts with which they enticed her out of her hiding place, she was singing strange, monotonous songs in her native tongue, which no one understood, and for some reason she is pleased.

The stream of vital young life had obviously transported her, and she seemed to have rejuvenated among them on this night. She was really here because of Tetiana. Tetiana wished to conjure up her future by the stream, and this was her wish as well. That is why she is happy.

In a loud voice she answers all the questions of the girls who are eager for even a moment's look into their unknown future, and she laughs merrily all the while.

The girls settle into their places at last, each according to her preference and will, and singing, begin to remove their beribboned, flowered wreaths from their heads and throw them, one after another, onto the glittering waters of the river. Then they wait.

When the first of the wreaths hit the water, the first voice was heard:

> Hey, on St. John's Eve, hey on Kupalo's Eve hey, hey, hey!
> A beautiful maid her fortune was seeking, hey, hey, hey!
> Flowers she picked for a wreath to plait,
> To throw in the water to predict her fate.

A second voice chimed in:

Flow my wreath on the glimmering waves,
Flow by the homestead where my loved one lives,
The wreath flowed downward on the stream,
Bearing the girl's heart with it.

Then a third:

Down the stream it disappeared slowly,
The girl's future Kupalo did not reveal,
Hey, on St. John's Eve, hey on Kupalo's Eve,
The girl at midnight went herbs a-digging,
Dug them at midnight, then boiled in a trice,
Fed them as poison before the sunrise.

After throwing the wreaths into the water, the girls follow them anxiously as they bounce on the merry waves. Will they take their wreaths far or near? To the loved one, or to a stranger? On what side of the shoreline will they stop? Here, in this village, or will they be pulled apart by the play of the waves, without realizing the goal destined for them?

A deep and anxious silence reigns for some time. The girls stand bending over the stream, with their eyes, indeed with their whole bodies, following the wreaths swaying in the water—only here and there a voice repeats:

Hey, on St. John's Eve, hey on Kupalo's Eve
A beautiful maid her fortune was seeking!
Flowers she picked for a wreath to plait,
To throw in the water to predict her fate.

Suddenly there are shouts and laughter.

One of the wreaths has been caught by a swifter wave near the shore and thrown playfully up on the grass. Two others, poorly braided, have floated apart into individual flowers throughout the stream, and soon disappear from sight.

Only Tetiana stands silent, unconcerned about anyone else, interested in nothing.

Deep in thought she pauses on the bank by the tranquil depths around the mighty boulder. She was trailed like a second shadow by the gypsy fortune-teller.

Tetiana's wreath is her main concern, what will happen to it? Where will the river take it? Toward the handsome Hryts into the mountains, or will it be thrown up on the river bank? Will it be torn to pieces, so that people will laugh at her? This is what concerns her at this moment.

But Tetiana does not remove her wreath from her head. She hesitates. Above all, she does not want anyone to see her throwing it in the water, does not want to sing and attract attention to herself. In a word, she doesn't want anything. She wants to do nothing that anyone else would want to participate in.

She wants something strictly for herself.

Now suddenly she does not even seem to want that.

She stands there, irresolute.

While hesitating, her thoughts turn to Hryts, and she asks herself: will they marry this fall as he has promised, or will they continue waiting?

"By the time the snow falls you will be in my house," he had told her. It came from his own lips and she believed him, him alone in the whole world. A wreath and water will tell her no more than he did—he, with his own voice, his own lips, that had kissed her....

"Do you want to throw your wreath in at this spot?" Mavra's voice behind her asks suddenly, interrupting her train of thought.

"Not here!" replies Tetiana involuntarily, and turns away, unpleasantly affected by the gypsy who has interrupted her thoughts.

"No, not here, daughter, not here," Mavra agrees, "see, there's an eddy here and it won't let the wreath flow freely. It will turn it around in the same spot. Go a little further and throw your wreath while thinking of your love and whether you will marry this fall or not."

"We'll marry, we'll marry!" Tetiana answers confidently, and adds irritably, "I'll throw my wreath wherever I want to," and with these words she steps away from the gypsy. She wants to throw the wreath so no one will see her, all by herself. Mavra is stopping her.

"Throw it wherever you wish, child, wherever you want!" says Mavra conciliatingly, but does not move away.

This further irritated the stubborn girl, who could not tolerate anyone telling her what to do, and she moved further away from the gypsy. She had not gone far, when some invincible power seemed to move her back to the place where she had left. She returned and took the wreath from her head. Then, without uttering a word, she threw the wreath with all her might into the water by the boulder.... The wreath twirled violently and in a few moments, floating into quieter waters, it began to move forward imperceptibly.

But not far.

Tetiana stood bent over the shoreline, her eyes wide, without moving a hair. Behind her stood the gypsy, doubled over.

A difficult moment ... silence....

"Oh-h-h!" cried Tetiana suddenly and stretched out her arms over the stream in panic. The wreath had floated into the centre where it was swept into an eddy. There it was twirled around in one spot for a minute or two, as if a plaything, and then it was suddenly pulled down into the river's bed and Tetiana saw it no more.

She turned silently, her face pale, toward the gypsy who was also standing motionless, her eyes gaping wide with fear, looking at the water. Now she looked at the girl with concern.

"He won't marry you this fall, your lad," she said, finally, and without thinking long, "he won't marry you."

Tetiana turned away.

"You don't say!" she declared haughtily, and glanced with lowered lids over the water.

"You don't believe me, child?" asked Mavra, with obvious rebuke.

"You don't say!" answered the girl haughtily, as before, in an unrecognizable voice, and, turning away from the river, she left.

* * *

Again some time passed.

Nastia left with her parents on a pilgrimage to distant parts and did not bid Hryts farewell. Her heart was aching from his neglect for nearly the entire summer. He had rarely visited her. But she did not reveal her pain to him, waiting patiently until he returned to her once again of his own volition, as this had happened many a time in the past, when anything separated them for a time. That he might be interested in another girl had not occurred to her yet. Of course, it was his restless nature that took over from time to time, and removed him from the house for long or short periods, or drove him to heated, enthusiastic labour; then it would be weeks before he came to see her.

But even during these times, he would drop in for a moment or two, make an appearance, ask a few questions, especially when the weather had turned bad while he was at work; at least furtively he would turn to her.

But this summer he appeared only occasionally in the evenings, and only for a minute. On Sundays it was as if the wind had swept him away.

"Where does he go?" Nastia asked herself and wondered.

But maybe he didn't go anywhere at all?

That was one thing. Another thing that troubled her was why he never told her, as he had in the past, where he had been after being away for a time.

For a long time now they have promised themselves to each other and are waiting for their parent's consent for the wedding to take place. And now he is beginning to neglect her. At just this very time. Her heart ached, foretelling sadness, and there were moments when she grieved bitterly at his ingratitude and indifference, at his strange character, and sometimes, during discussions with her mother, she even wept.

She thought once of going to a gypsy fortune-teller about whose powers she had heard, as though in a fairytale, but she was afraid. She was also ashamed. She had heard that the fortune-teller lived all alone on Chabanytsia Mountain, in the forest, so she would have to go with someone.

But she had no one with whom she could go. And even if she went, she said to herself, what would she say to her? That her love had broken his word? She did not really know if he had. He had assured her many a time that he loved only her—her alone in the entire world.

So what can she ask her? Find out what? That he does not like to stay at home for long, or in any one place? She is already used to this. He has been like this since birth. But that is what a fortune-teller is for—who knows if she can help. Unless, perhaps, someone has cast a spell on him?

Who?

She does not know.

Some girl?

Which one?

All the girls in the village knew that they were promised to each other, none of them would step between them, unless it were some young married woman. She is not afraid of them, although people say that there are some among them that drive a man mad. But he is not afraid. Hryts is not timid. In the whole village he alone is afraid of nothing. Then why go to a fortune-teller?

So Nastia mused and remained at home. She did not go. Only after her parents began to discuss a pilgrimage to a distant place did she beg to go with them. She wanted to pray to God, repent her sins, plead for happiness. And she went. Without telling any of her friends, she gathered her things and went off.

Hryts felt confused when he heard that Nastia had gone with her parents on such a long journey without having said a word to him, nor even bidding him good-bye.

Suddenly he felt remorseful and sorry for the good, kind girl who had never said a word of reproach all summer for his inattention to her.

True, he had not always been indifferent to her, only since he had begun to meet Tetiana—only then did he begin to neglect her. After every meeting with Tetiana, he seemed to lose control of himself, so deeply had she entered his heart and soul. He would have married her long ago if he could. She drove all common sense out of his head, as he often told her himself, and with her every word she bound him to her, like a silk thread being wound around a finger. But now that he had not seen Nastia for some time, because his father had chained him to some work, he began to miss her and clearly felt that he could not do without her. How good she was, so accommodating, so agreeable to everything he desired, and now, suddenly, she had turned away from him. He had only himself to blame. Himself alone. She had always been the same—loved no one but him....

"Hryts," she had threatened him the last time he saw her, smiling jestingly at him after not seeing him for some time and saying: "You must have found yourself another Nastia since you're forgetting your first one. If you have, then beware!" But saying this she pulled him toward her and embraced him warmly. "I'll find myself another Hryts," she continued, "the world doesn't end with our village. You know there are many lads out there, not only Hryts, if this is what you wish." She had laughed then, gazing into his eyes, embracing and fondling him until he, too, laughed, and they reconciled.

So it had always been. The same, good, indulgent Nastia, who was cunning as a vixen. It was hard not to love her. Her eyes, blue as the sky, were always merry, they had never shown anger, her lips always greeted him with a smile.

Now she had gone on a pilgrimage—without saying a word. For the first time in her life, it seemed, she had truly felt aggrieved at him. Could she have heard about Turkynia? he thought uncomfortably. Heavens! If she had found out, who could have told her? Better he should tell her everything himself when she comes back. At least it would be the truth. She will learn everything from him, and if she becomes angry, he will apologize to her. She is intelligent, she will forgive him, and they will restore harmony as they had done in the past many a time. She is good for him, like a piece of bread, like balm on a wound. With her he can do everything. He cannot give her up, he has loved her for a long time.

Thus he reasons.

He cannot leave one because he has loved her for a long time, is even promised to her; the other he cannot forsake, his heart will not permit him. So let them make up their minds between the two of them, if they don't like it....

* * *

When Nastia returned from the pilgrimage Hryts went to her at once. His waiting had not been in vain.

A seemingly different person came out to him—she was tall, fine, but somehow thin.

He looked at her and his conscience smote him. He was to blame for everything.

Why hadn't she told him she was going on a pilgrimage, he asked in greeting her. He might have joined them. He would have gone too. Why did she keep it a secret from him?

Has she become indifferent to him? Does she not love him any more?

In answer, Nastia burst into tears.

She loves him, as she always has, but he is unkind, has been avoiding her. It is inconsiderate of him to do this. Why not be truthful and tell her where he has been going, she will forgive him and all will be as it has always been between them. Besides, she told him seriously, he must send the matchmakers, because her parents do not wish to wait any longer. "On account of that Hryts," they say "the one who chases after the wind, she will be left with a grey braid." She assured him that she had gone on the pilgrimage out of grief at his actions, to pray herself away from him and her sins. She's telling him this for the last time. Now he must confess. Is he thinking about another? Does he love another? If he does, then so be it.

Hryts pulls her into his embrace and holds her against his heart.

"If I tell you, what will happen?"

"That which must, don't worry about that," she answers, "just tell me."

"Well," he says, hesitatingly, "do you know Ivanykha Dub's daughter, Tetiana, from the third village over? The one with dark brows, the richest girl around. She loves me."

Nastia turned pale.

"Turkynia?"

"Turkynia."

"The one with the gold half-moon earrings, who measures with her eyebrows."

"The very same, who measures with her eyebrows."

"She has caught hold of *you*, Hryts?" she barely speaks.

"Loves me to death."

"And you?"

Hryts laughingly pulls her into his arms again.

"I love both of you. One of you is blue-eyed, the other black-browed. Both of you are girls, but Nastia is not *Turkynia*."

Nastia turned grave as never before.

"Hryts," she asks, "are you of two minds that you love both of us, wooing both of us, deceiving both of us? But know this!" her blue eyes glittered, "you will not abandon Nastia, you will not make a fool of Nastia!"

"So far I haven't made a fool of either of you," Hryts says defensively, "because I haven't sent matchmakers to either yet."

"But you knew where to find me when you felt like telling me you loved me?"

"I knew, Nastia, and I know it now," he answers, "but I'm sorry for Turkynia. She'll start lamenting. She'll curse me and you, too. What should we do about it?"

"We'll get married," says Nastia decisively, and suddenly, like a great serpent, embraces Hryts.

"But Turkynia, Nastia? I don't want to kill her. Like you, she truly loves me."

Nastia lowered her eyes, frowning, then, as though she had mulled something, said:

"Don't worry about her. I'll take care of her, I'll deal with her, so that everything will turn out well, so she won't curse us—neither you nor me."

Hryts looked in wonder at Nastia who stood close to him, almost touching him with her breasts. She was once again the same as before, good and supportive, knowing exactly what to do, when he did not. She had not changed. She was sensible about everything.

"What will you do with her?" he finally asked, somewhat timidly.

Nastia burst into laughter. Then falling silent, she threw both arms about his neck, gazing deeply into his eyes with her glittering blue eyes, eyes that he loved, and asked him:

"Do you love Turkynia very much, Hryts?"

Hryts pushed her away.

"Leave me alone, Nastia," he answered angrily, irritated by something that he sensed in her voice. "Do what you will, but leave me in peace. Now that I've told you everything, give me peace...."

"And Turkynia?"

"Kill her, if she's in your way. I won't"

"And I won't either, Hryts," answered Nastia, laughing heartily, her white teeth gleaming, "I won't either, Hryts."

"Then do what you will. You are both alike. Just leave me alone."

"We are both alike, you say, so then it's all the same to you, which one you marry. I've been yours for a long time.... You said so yourself, so you won't abandon me now, make a fool of me...."

"And Turkynia?" Hryts asked again.

Nastia contorted her mouth in contempt.

"Don't worry about her," she said shortly, "I won't kill her."

"And I won't either, Nastia. So what will you do with her?" asked Hryts anxiously.

Something glimmered again in Nastia's eyes, turning green, and like before, she burst into laughter.

Hryts fell into a rage.

"Why are you laughing again? This is no laughing matter."

"It is for me," answered Nastia. "Be sensible, Hryts," she advised him, changing abruptly to her usual serious and calm demeanor which always gained an upper hand over him, over his dual character, "Do you really think that you're the only one in the world? That if she doesn't marry you, she won't find another? God help us, if everyone thought like you!"

Hryts was silent.

"Yes, she'll find another," he said, finally, "but she'll curse us, and complain."

"Who, Hryts? Turkynia?" asks Nastia. "Don't tell me you're afraid of her?... Who will curse us?" she repeats, at the same time her voice pre-empting what he will say next.

"Ivanykha Dub," answers Hryts, "you don't joke with her...."

"Let her," answers Nastia indifferently. "I will repel her curses from us. You just tell me all you know about her."

Hryts became confused.

"What is there to say?... She's beautiful.... And that's it...."

"Is she really as rich as they say?"

"That's how people think of her. I didn't count her flocks of sheep, didn't drive her cattle to water either. They say she's the richest person in the village, so she must be."

"Yes, yes, Hryts, but don't worry," Nastia began again, soothingly, "She'll get married without you."

"I know she'll get married. I'm just sorry to have to say so."

Nastia straightened up ... and she was tall.

"But you're not sorry for me?" she asked in a voice that shook on the verge of tears, and with the bitterness that had long burned in her heart.

"Of course, I'm sorry," Hryts soothed her, "I am sorry, my cuckoo. I'm even sorry for myself that I love both of you, and have neither. I would take one and not leave the other. I would love one and caress the other. I would woo one and marry the other," and with these words he began to laugh strangely, "What should I do?"

"Don't love both of us."

"Then don't the two of you love me! Leave me, Nastia! Why are you holding on to me? If you leave me, I'll marry Tetiana...."

Nastia burst into tears.

"Aren't you afraid of God, talking this way?" she asked, sobbing, "What kind of a heart do you have?"

"We will all stand before God one day. Tetiana Dub, you and I. Hush! Don't cry, Nastia. Do you hear me? Tetiana, you and I! And He will be the judge. Hush, don't cry," he consoled her, putting his arms around her. "How can I help what has happened? Did I want this? So it was fated, or perhaps predicted for me." This last he said with a smile, but Nastia did not notice.

"Why did you go to Turkynia when you already had me?"

"Because she bewitched me," he answered. "She is an enchantress, the most beautiful in the village. She enticed me with her dark eyes, her dark brows, the red poppies with which she adorned her hair.... She blinded my soul and senses. What do you want? That's why I'm a man, that's why I have a heart.... Hush, don't cry! I haven't died yet. When I have, and you become a widow, then cry to your heart's content, but for now, I want you to smile. If you don't want to smile, then at least love me as you once did, otherwise I'll leave you and go to Tetiana. She does not cry."

Nastia was shaken to the core by these words, but she stopped crying and wiped her tears.

"I do love you, Hryts.... You are mine," she said, coming close and embracing him fondly, like before. "We are betrothed, Hryts.... You hear?" she asked entreatingly, her eyes anxious, yet threatening. "We are betrothed. You won't make a fool of me...."

"I heard you. When are you going to stop?" Hryts was annoyed. "I've told you all I know and the truth, now let me be. What do you want from me? That I should leave home and go who knows where? That wouldn't be hard—I'll go."

Nastia again flings her arms about his neck.

"Not to leave home, Hryts," she soothed like a sleepwalker, "but to marry me, Hryts...."

"Then we'll marry ... but...," and he stopped suddenly, pushing the girl away, afraid of her determination.

oop

"Never go out to meet Turkynia again," she commands him gravely and piercing him sharply with bright eyes, darkened now by her inner turmoil, "lest we not marry because of her. She'll find another. She won't die without you, she's rich, Hryts, but I...," she stopped, her eyes again filling with tears, and hid her face in her hands.

Vary

"Don't be afraid, and stop crying," Hryts says soothingly. "Am I abandoning you?... I won't go to meet Turkynia again. You don't believe me? Perhaps because I said she was the most beautiful girl in the village? It's true. She is beautiful, there's no denying it," he declares with finality, hiding a smile under his moustache. "Don't be afraid."

Nastia's eyes began to glitter.

"Hryts," she waved a hand threateningly, "you're not fooling me. I'm saying it again, don't go out to meet that Dub girl any more."

Hryts turned away from her, silent, and walking a few steps away from her, called out:

"Goodbye for now!"

She did not reply, but making up her mind suddenly, rushed impetuously after him:

"You won't go to meet her?"

He paused. "I won't."

"You've got to end it, Hryts!"

"Yes, I must."

"I'll end it. Just make sure you don't see her, and don't worry about the rest."

"I'm not worrying," he answered. "You worry. You are all alike. Leave me in peace...." And with that he strides away.

"Hryts, I'm preparing the wedding towels," she called out after him.

"Prepare them for this fall...."

"But the fall is already here."

"Well then, that's fine."

"If not, Hryts, I'll drown myself, I'll die!" Nastia complains and threatens.

"Don't be afraid," he said, and paused. "You won't die, I'll probably die sooner...."

"I won't give you up, Hryts...."

"You don't say!" said Hryts, then falling silent, continued on his way.

* * *

Once again old Andronati wandered into the village where Hryts lived with his parents, and was now circling the village for a second time, begging alms. And again, as she usually did, blue-eyed Nastia gave him more than anyone else. She loved to give him alms because he gave thanks with such sincerity and eloquence. He knew how to speak to the heart so well that one could listen to his words forever.

So it was this time.

After thanking and blessing her at least ten times and bowing to the lovely young woman a number of times, for if it was not enough that she was so generous in her gifts, she herself had opened the gate for him today, so he would not have any bother. Looking closely at her, he begins to wonder at last why she is tarrying with him, seeing him off and chattering away in a friendly fashion, exhorting him to take special care of his old feet in the mountains, because the mountains are hard on those who are not accustomed to climbing their heights.

She chatters thus, then stops abruptly. Standing still for a moment, she finally sits down and asks him to sit as well.

The old man was surprised, but does not sit down. He only leaned on his cane and looks at her. How good and kind she is, this girl, how compassionate! It isn't only today, either, but ever since he has known her. She has always been like that. "God bless you! God bless you!" he repeats again and again, preparing to walk away. But Nastia gets up and detains him.

"Grandpa," she says, "I have something I wish to talk to you about today. Whether you sit or stand, I must say it."

Astonished, the old man replies: "Then tell me, child, what it is you need, or want to know, but it's better that I stand. I've already become so accustomed to standing on my feet that it doesn't bother me."

"Grandpa Andronati," began Nastia, aiming her bright eyes high up at the mountain tops as if collecting her thoughts, "you know me well, Grandpa, me and the Donchuk's son Hryts, with whom you have talked many times and not for the first time today. You know my parents and you know his. Please listen to what I have to say, and once I say it, I have a request to make of you."

"Go ahead, tell me, my heart, my dove," answers the old man, leaning more heavily on his cane and looking at the girl with grave attention, so as

not to miss a word of what she has to say. She is so compassionate and blue-
eyed. A good child, there is no question. She had never sent him away from
her home with empty hands, and when others looked at him with suspicion
and sometimes would not even allow him into their yards, very often she
would offer him a corner in which to spend the night.

"We have loved each other a long time, Donchuk's son Hryts and I,
Grandpa Andronati, as you yourself may have guessed," confesses the girl.

The old man smiled.

"This is news!" he said, then quickly added with frank warmth, "Who
wouldn't love that lad! I've wandered much of the world, but have never met
a handsomer, livelier lad than this Hryts. He looks like St. George himself
when he is mounted on his horse. Handsome he is, and proud, God bless him,
but he is also good and intelligent and soft-hearted." With these words the old
man began laughing again, as if recalling something. "He is also attracted to
the pretty ones, am I not right, my dove?" he asks, still laughing.

"Yes and no, Grandpa," answers Nastia hesitantly.

"That is the problem, my white dove."

"Hryts has truly loved only me...."

"How do you know how boys love in this world?" he interrupts, "and
especially those like your Hryts? One, or a few?"

"Because he told me this himself."

The old man whistled through his teeth as though in amazement and
laughed again.

"Then what's your worry if, as you say, he loves you?" he asks. "Or has
he stopped loving you and is planning to send matchmakers to another?"

"Oh no, Grandpa," answers Nastia impatiently, "Hryts is not like that. The
trouble is something else and you can advise us."

"Me? How can I help you?" he asked. "Where are your parents—your
father and mother? Is it that they don't want you to get married?"

"That's not it either, Grandpa. They are not against it. We will marry ...
but...," and she stopped.

"But what?" he asks more animatedly. "What is it you need me for? I am
old and poor, I live on people's kindness, on people's alms."

"True, Grandpa," answers Nastia sympathetically, "but if you could help
us this time, once we're married we'll take you in to live with us. You'll stay
with us to the end; we'll look after you as long as God wills it."

The old man laughed heartily.

"That's what you say, young woman," he retorts, "but no sooner than you
are married you won't want to know me!"

"Oh no, Grandpa," Nastia defends herself, laughing at the old man's disbelief. "We are not like that. I'm not wicked like that, nor is Hryts. You yourself said that he is kind-hearted. Then believe me."

"Then what is this all about?" asks the old man, now genuinely interested. "Do you need some special herb, perhaps? I have none with me right now. I would have to pick them.

"No, no, not herbs, Grandpa, only your ancient wisdom and words."

"Wo-rds? A-ha!" he drawled with astonishment.

"Words, Grandpa, and wisdom...."

"Then tell me, so I'll know."

"Grandpa," Nastia begins again and sighs deeply, as if preparing for a heavy burden. "Grandpa," and her voice and lips trembled, "listen. Beyond Chabanytsia, past the White Rock, as it is called, lives a mill-owner, a widow, named Ivanykha Dub. She is a devout woman, the richest in the village, but she is charitable to the poor. This I know about her. But she has a daughter, an only daughter, Grandpa, spoiled like a bird, and people call her Turkynia."

"A-ha!" the old man drawled his words as if suddenly remembering something, then fell silent and waited.

"Grandpa, this Turkynia, as she is called in the village, is an enchantress and has somehow bound Hryts to her. She has taken his heart, probably with evil herbs, her dark brows, and is now standing in our way. We have already received the matchmakers and we're betrothed, but Hryts's heart is still restless. He embraces me, but loves Turkynia; he kisses me, but yearns for her. He can't forget her. He dreams about her constantly, always with red poppies, with tender words. Save us, Grandpa!" begged the girl, her hands clasped as though in prayer. "You know Hryts, he is tender-hearted, he'll swing between the both of us. All because of her, because of her dark brows, her evil herbs, her inducements."

Having said this, Nastia fell silent, as though she had fainted on her feet. The old man was sunk deep in deep thought.

"You say she's very beautiful?" he asks after a few minutes.

"Beautiful, like a princess. Dark-browed, Hryts says. Her eyes bewitch like a bright star in the heavens, she bewitches him with her flowers. What am I to do, Grandpa? Help me!"

"And you say she is rich?"

"The richest in the village."

"And her mother is a devout woman?"

"Like a nun."

"Charitable to the poor?"

"That I don't really know. They say she is very kind, but also very strict. Like a lady, they say."

"And the daughter bewitches?" he asked in disbelief.

"With her eyebrows and herbs, with red blossoms that she always wears in her hair she binds him to her.... Oh, Grandpa!" she added desperately. "Help me!"

"What advice do you want from me, child?" asks the old man again and once more falls into deep reflection about Hryts. It would be a shame to lose this fair girl's friendship. He was sorry, too, for Hryts, to be torn between the two. His Mavra, too, had loved two men and in the end had forfeited her destiny.

The old man sighed and leaned even harder on his cane.

"Tell me what I should do and I'll do it. But I have no herbs. I cannot pick them any more. Maybe I should say an incantation? That is one thing I still know how to do. I'll turn Turkynia away with words. I can't do anything else, my age won't permit me.... If only I had Mavra...."

Nastia was revitalized. Her eyes, blue as the skies and usually kind and merry, suddenly gleamed with a peculiar green glow. She said:

"I'll teach you, Grandpa. I've already thought of how we can frighten her into letting Hryts go. You'll help me. Are you not sorry to see Hryts wasting his future, marrying me—but grieving for her? First I'll threaten her through you ... and if that doesn't help.... I know where to go.... On Chabanytsia Mountain there is a fortune-teller who gives good advice.... I'll go to her. But you go first, talk sternly to her. Will you go, Grandpa?" she begs.

The old man considered.

"Will you invite an old man to your wedding then?" He was negotiating a bit, but his thoughts were really with Hryts.

"Oh, Grandpa, of course you must come! Just tell Turkynia what I said, give her a good fright, tell her what I told you and add your own words."

"Then tell me what to say, little dove," said the old man. "I will do anything for Hryts's happiness, and when I say my word, it will be said, and when I pronounce a curse, then it will be pronounced. Once and for all may Hryts have peace!"

"Yes, Grandpa," Nastia agreed hastily and repeated, "once and for all may Hryts have peace!..."

"Then tell me, my dove, so that I can do what you wish," the old man said again.

Nastia straightened up, took a deep breath, and began:

"Find Turkynia, Grandpa, beg for alms and after blessing her, say this:

'Turkynia, I have heard that you love Hryts, the finest lad on the Hungarian border; that you have bewitched him with flowers and words; that you cause misfortune, take away happiness.

'And I have heard, Turkynia, that Hryts does not love you, because he has long loved another. He has chosen blue-eyed Nastia for his own and will soon be marrying her.

'What do you want from him, beautiful Tetiana? That he should leave his young bride-to-be and take you? Why, you'll be cursed, not only by his bride, but by all the people who will hear about you. You will be a laughing-stock and jeered at by the whole village, left in sadness like a phantom.

'And I have heard, Turkynia, that you are wealthy, so you will be able to find another. I'm telling you, Hryts's bride-to-be weeps and sorrows because of you, curses you bitterly. Hryts loved her before he saw you, he caressed you while wooing her. That is why he is taking her as his wife and will not be sending his matchmakers to woo you.

'Turkynia, I have heard all that I am saying from the girl whom Hryts will marry. He himself has complained to her about you, that you are to blame, that you have bewitched him, turned his head.

'With your dark brows you seemed to admire him, and on the other hand, you affected his mind. You adorned yourself with red poppies to lure him, wandered the forest playing with its echoes, and thus you led him astray....

'Now come to your senses. He is renouncing you, fearing your black brows, he loves fair ones. He will not meet you any more, so do not wait, unless you happen to see him on his black horse somewhere. Then you must turn away from him, so people won't know that you loved him, took him away from another.

'As I've already said, Hryts has long had Nastia, he thinks of you no more, Turkynia. He has stopped loving you, sorceress, and will come to you no more. Bid him farewell....'

"So, Grandpa," ended Nastia in a rush, and sighing deeply, as though released from a heavy burden, she turned away.

The old man stood silent for a long moment, as if reflecting on what she had told him, then spoke up:

"Better now than too late." But suddenly remembering Mavra, he was saddened. After another moment of reflection, he added:

"I won't tell her right away what you want me to say, child. I'll wait until the third banns have been announced, so that the witch won't have time to stop the wedding. Dark brows have always wrought harm and he who does know what cure to use against them will perish, as though in the depths of hell. God be praised, my child, that you are blue-eyed and do no harm, only good. I will relay all your words to her and add those that I know on my own. Let her travel her own road and not stop Hryts on his path to happiness. I pray for him, I have done this for a long time. He is like my own kin, I will do anything for him. Don't worry about anything any more, my good children, unless it's about a nice wedding. And invite the poor to it, too. Don't forget an old man. He will sing for you about where Hryts comes from, why he is here, and why I am here. God grant you happiness, my blue-eyed child. Look after Hryts, keep him away from her. Make your eyes sparkle the way she does, and if he's tender-hearted, as we know he is, he'll go after you and forget her. The old man will do his bit, he'll turn Tetiana Dub away—stand on guard for Hryts's happiness—and all will be well."

Andronati then nodded to the girl and, saying no more, turned and went away. Nastia ran swiftly back into the house and began to work while singing a song....

* * *

It was three or four weeks before the second fall feastday of the Blessed Virgin Mary. At his father's request, Hryts again prepared to go to the neighbouring village on family matters. This time he decided to ride his horse over Chabanytsia Mountain along the White Path. It was a good few weeks since he had come here to meet Tetiana. Somehow there did not seem to be time, for his father kept him at work, as though he had clapped him in irons, and secondly—he was afraid of Nastia. In spite of all her goodness and consideration, ever since she had found out about Tetiana she was ready to run after him all the way here, in order to prevent him from seeing her....

Riding along now, step by step, he thought about the two girls.

How will it all end?

He must wed Nastia. He has already sent matchmakers to her parents. He still does not know what will happen with Tetiana. His wedding will be held after the second feastday of the Virgin Mary and Tetiana knows nothing about it. She is waiting for matchmakers from him.

He has not seen her for some time now.

In truth, he has ridden here a few times in secret, but lately it so happened that when she would come into the forest he would be at work. When he would set out again secretly into the forest to meet her, her mother needed her at home and she would not come. So their paths slowly diverged despite their love for each other. Only God knows whether this isn't for the best, although he loves her ... he loves her.... How he loves her! But in vain....

But he will see her again, although Nastia is against it. It does not trouble him that he has given Nastia his word that he will never see her again. What will be, will be, one can still love. He is marrying Nastia.... But Tetiana?

"Tetiana?" repeated some inner voice that reminded him of Nastia's voice, and then was silent.

What will he do with her?

He cannot marry both. Let the two of them come to some agreement between themselves now that the situation has taken this turn. Nastia can do it, she said she would. She is inventive, she has a solution for everything. She loves him, knows about Turkynia. Let her take care of it. She won't kill her.... How can he help her now? Start a fight? All girls are alike, they contribute to misfortune, then cry and worry themselves sick.

What use are they to him?

Could any good come of this perhaps? Hryts grew serious and sighed.

What is good in this for him? That he loves two at the same time? The only satisfaction he had was when he was in the forest with Turkynia, who loved him truly. It was like being in paradise, but had this lasted long? Nastia suddenly came between them and it was as though everything had turned to stone—everything had ended. Nastia was good and generous to him, he did not know a finer girl. It wasn't that he had suddenly stopped loving her and begun to love Turkynia. No. Tetiana Dub had wormed her way into his heart and soul and he cannot forget her....

But what can he do about her now?

About her mother?

Ivanykha Dub does not jest.

If only they could meet some place, quickly smile at each other, the heart would be eased no matter what happened later—but this way....

And then what?

"What then?" he asked himself and could find no answer.

Somehow it will be resolved, the sensible Nastia has said. She is beautiful and rich, she'll get married without you. Why worry about it?

True.

Why should he worry about it?

Even girls can be sensible. Let them worry about it. They, too, loved. Tetiana had also loved.

Why has she hidden from him now? Has she learned of his wedding with Nastia?

Maybe she has found out....

Ah, Turkynia, my little bird, what kind of heart do you have?...

Riding thus, he reflects on himself and the girls. Passing familiar spots along the White Path, he looks longingly to the left into the deep ravine, then to the right up Chabanytsia with its White Rock, where they had also met.

For some reason his heart is full of expectation that Tetiana will appear from somewhere—proud, smiling, adorned in her red flowers, and say as usual: "Here I am."

But although he looks about eagerly and no matter how much he wishes for peace "with her," "she" does not appear. She does not appear and her voice is not heard.

Hryts sighs mournfully, his brows knitted together in a deep frown. She should have come, his heart says, for he is here. Of course, he had not sent matchmakers as he promised, he was not going to marry her, he would sadden her heart, but who is really to blame for this? He alone?

Both of them are to blame....

That's why she should come, should love him always. Be here.... Be as she had been.... At least once more.... Once....

"Tur-ky-nia!" He did not even realize that he had shouted.

"Tur-ky-nia!" The echo flew across to the opposite forest-covered mountain and died away.

"Are you *here*?" He called out again with indescribable longing in his voice and waited.

"*Here*," came the answering echo faintly in his own voice and was silent.

In spite of his listening and turning at every rustle, despite his longing, there was no movement, no response....

Hryts sank into deep thought and waited no more.

He knew now that he would not see her.

She must have learned that he had proposed to another and is not coming out, she is crying....

*   *   *

Riding along in deep thought, Hryts did not notice how the sky had imperceptibly darkened with heavy clouds. A cool wind began to rock the tree-tops and thunder rolled ominously, followed by lightning flashes. This went on continuously until Hryts's black horse grew wild with terror and began to stamp and leap about violently.

"This animal foresees misfortune with its restlessness," thinks Hryts, and begins to look about for some shelter.

The sky is menacing, covered with dark clouds.

The forest grows darker and large drops of rain begin to fall. At first they come singly, then thicker and stronger. He spurs his horse to greater speed and the animal responds with long leaps up the White Path while the crashing thunder shakes the entire mountain, as if rolling down its steep hillsides, and finally stopping and dying away.

It seems that the rain is falling on Hryts twice. Once, so it seemed, from the torn clouds, and a second time from the fir branches. Riding quickly, he continues looking for a spot where he can find shelter and calm his horse, who is frightened by the thunder and lightning. The narrow White Path curling around Chabanytsia, and often right on the edge of the ravine, was now awash with water, and the swift horse, dashing up the mountainside, kept slipping and sliding on it.

It was dangerous to be riding right above the gorge on a frightened horse. Hryts finally managed to stop him, dismount, and lead him by the bridle, while continuing to look for shelter.

In the deep abyss the rising water of the river boils and rages through the broadening stream, breaking off the shoreline and carrying everything with it.

Here and there small rocks and pebbles, uprooted by the strength of the downpour, rattle down the mountainside and disappear in the waters below.

Suddenly Hryts stops.

On a small incline that looked as if the mountain had heaved out of itself, and was shielded completely by the thick branches of the firs that grew around it, there stands, or rather hides, a small mountain cottage, ancient and lopsided.

The White Path along which Hryts is travelling runs right past it. Although it does not stop at the cottage doorway, but continues up the mountain and perhaps down and around it—he does not know—at least the cottage offers shelter.

Hidden there, the cottage seems to be leaning over the ravine with a crooked window in one wall and an equally crooked door on another.

Hryts immediately decides to stop here and stay until the storm boiling over the mountain and forest has spent itself, then go on.

Having made up his mind, he ties his horse on the quieter side of the house and approaches the door.

Since he is tall he must bend down, because the doorway is low and crooked. Here he is suddenly startled.

At the very same moment as he was opening the door from the outside, it was opened by someone from inside and before he realized what was happening, he was face to face with an old gypsy woman, who seemed to have emerged from the earth. Grey, dishevelled, with brilliant black eyes, she stood there smiling at him.

"Come in, son, come in," she invited him with a diffidence that hid a secret fear and uncertainty. "Come in. I have been expecting you for more than a year. The cards predicted it," and stepping aside to let him enter, she pressed against the smoke-blackened wall to give him room.

Hryts, unexpectedly seeing a frightful, spectre-like gypsy woman, hesitated at first, but glancing again at her face and her eyes in which was reflected such a great sadness that he was deeply moved, he stepped forward more confidently.

Some smoke from the stove struck him disagreeably in the face after the fresh forest air outdoors. He stood stooped for a moment, looking around. On his rides he had never come as far as this cottage, even when meeting Tetiana several times during the summer, until the storm had led him here today. What misery! What poverty! Some colourful old rags, two gypsy sacks, a cane, a small chest of some kind loaded down with fresh herbs; an old, almost empty, smoke-blackened sideboard with a piece of bread. Hanging on a rod under the roof was an ancient red shawl, which was not usual apparel in the local villages; beside it were a few wreaths of dried mushrooms. A bench stood beside the clay oven stove and on it was a black cat, black as gypsy hair. Further up on the chimney funnel sat a large tame crow with glittering eyes—and that was all.

"Sit down in a poor gypsy woman's home, son, sit down," begs Mavra, at whose house Hryts had arrived. "Sit down, don't be proud. Here I am, a poor woman, alone in the whole forest where a human foot rarely finds its way to me. As you can see, I live as God wills it. I have what good people give me. If they don't, then I live on roots, like all our poor gypsies. That's how it is. Please sit down."

Hryts sat down, silent, staring at the gypsy who, for some reason, was bowing right to the ground before him, and reminding him of old Andronati who always did this. After a moment he rises and looks through the tiny glass that serves as a window.

"It's nothing, nothing," soothed Mavra. "It's still raining. Sit here a bit with a poor gypsy. Just look, here I am, completely alone on this whole mountain, in this whole forest. If someone comes along this path occasionally, I sometimes see a human face, and if not—then I don't. Do stay, son," she spoke quickly, gazing him straight in the eye, while her own eyes glittered brightly.

"It's been a long time since I've seen such a handsome prince as you," she continues, bowing humbly, as she had earlier. "Long, long ago," she sighed.

"Are you perhaps the gypsy of whom it is said that she knows herbs and how to tell fortunes?" asked Hryts suddenly, his eyes never leaving her face.

"As if I would know? There are many gypsies in this world. But I can tell fortunes, and how! There is no mystery that I cannot unravel. I tell it and how! I know all about herbs, too. Do you need any? For good or bad?" she asked in a wheedling manner. "Ha-i, ha-i," she sang out, "Ha-i, ha-i," and keeps staring closely at the young man.

Hryts began to feel uncomfortable from the gaze of those big black eyes, filled with sadness, as if they no longer had any point of support in the hut except his face. She seemed to be drinking him in.

"But I have heard," Hryts began again, "that this fortune-teller does not always live here, but keeps changing places. But I see that you have a house."

Mavra became frightened.

"No, son," she assured him, "I am the fortune-teller you heard about. There is no other in the district. No, there is no other—no other as unfortunate as Mavra, who ruined her entire young life in a foreign land, sick and out of her senses. She came to in a forest and was left to the kindness of good people." Saying this she burst into tears.

The gypsy woman began to pique Hryts's curiosity.

Outdoors the rain was pouring down without stopping; thunder was still rumbling across the sky and further travel was out of the question.

"How did you ruin your life?" he asked, and began to fill his pipe, at the same time handing a pinch of tobacco to the gypsy, who snatched it greedily, and immediately took out her own pipe.

"Ruined, son, ruined," she began, lighting her pipe and smoking.

"Looking at you now, I want to cry and laugh at the same time. Merciful God! It's been a long time since I've talked with a man about my misfortune, because it's rare that someone comes to see me here. And who wants to listen to a poor gypsy woman? They throw you some bread, like to a hungry dog, or a bit of flour, or a few pennies, then tell you to leave their house with a warning not to steal anything as you go." She said bitterly, "And even if I took anything, son—look at how poor I am and forsaken. Who will earn a livelihood for me? My cat?" She pointed at her black companion. "He can't earn. If it weren't for my sin, I would still be with my husband today. My husband was the chief of our clan, son. His name was Radu. And my father earned his bread by playing a violin. I was their only child."

Mavra began to cry again.

"And my mother, son, my mother," she sobbed, "what a dancer she was in her youth!" She shook her head in wonder. "And I was, too, son, very early in my youth, very early. When I danced for the gentry in Hungary, everything would begin shimmering before my eyes. And nearly always around a campfire. It was that cursed dance that ruined my life."

"What dance?" asked Hryts, bewildered.

"Why that dance that sometimes provides young gypsy girls with a livelihood along with their fortunetelling. Ah, that was some dance, son! See, I'll show you, so you'll remember where you've been."

And here old, grey-haired Mavra began to dance before the young man with light, graceful steps, almost on her toes, bending and turning gracefully, at the same time attempting to sing along.

Hryts watched the old woman for some time, silently and without blinking. As he watched, his heart became filled with inexpressible sorrow for this poor, forsaken woman who was trying to please him in the best way that she knew how. Panting and out of breath, she continued interpreting the dance that had earned her "bread" and that obviously had once been her pride and the misfortune of her indigent life....

He rose and turned to the window. Finishing her dance, she fell exhausted before him to the floor.

"This was the dance, son," she said, breathing heavily and sitting up while he took some coins out of his leather belt and threw them with a sympathetic gesture into her lap.

"This is the dance I performed in the Hungarian plain and in the towns, but longer than I did for you just now, because then I was young and healthy. It is called the csárdás. The gentry who travelled across the plain and past our camp would drop in on us and enjoy it. Other gypsy boys and girls besides me also danced. Afterwards Radu used to send me into a small town nearby for alms and fortune-telling—and that was the worst. Once ... twice ... and three times, son, until everything was at an end. After this we moved away from there. This was a long time ago, son, a long, long time ago, and Mavra was young and beautiful then...."

Hryts filled his pipe again and she, wondrously revitalized by his presence, continued talking:

"I would have a son like you today," she told him with an unexpectedly artless look in her beautiful, sad eyes, "if it hadn't been for a secret love and with it sin; sin betrays everything and that is why I am alone today, alone in the entire village, on this entire mountain, in this entire forest. May God never grant anyone such a fate as mine. No one worries about you, whether you are alive or dead. You live with the wild animals in the forest and no one else. I had parents," she began mechanically, out of habit, "and I lost them. I had a husband—he renounced and abandoned me; I had a child—a boy—he was killed or stolen—God only knows. I was left alone. Alone, son," she continued with large tears of grief in her eyes. "Alone, as I've already said, on this entire mountain, in this entire forest, unless, from time to time...," she stopped. At that moment a loud thunderclap struck the forest, interrupting her talk, and as if warned by it, she did not mention Tetiana of whom she was about to say that she was her only joy in the world. She returned to her earlier reminiscences about herself: "Alone, son, alone," she repeated, "unless the Lord sees fit to send me an angel, like you. You are my handsome prince!"

With these words she crossed her arms across her chest and bowed deeply and humbly before him, as if she were fitting her entire squandered life into the bow.... Never before, perhaps, had her poor soul, which had known only humiliation, sorrow and pain, luxuriated as it did in that moment, as she looked at this handsome young stranger with the beautiful blue eyes who was in her house. But where had she seen such eyes in her life before? Those eyes, this entire figure, this face? Where? Dear God! Something strange is happening in her poor soul. She begins to cry and does not know why. Then she begins laughing and also does not know why. She only knows that he is the reason—he, who with his looks, had revived memories in her soul of her youth and her past. Therefore she must cry and laugh.

"Come and visit me again, son," of all the strange emotions that shook her, she is only able to say these words. "Come visit me, prince!" she begs from the depths of her soul and crossing her arms again, once more she bows humbly to the ground to him. "Come visit a poor woman! You will be her heavenly angel. Long ago my cards told me that two men would come to my house. One has already been here, in the winter, and I didn't receive him in my house, because I was afraid. And now you—the second one—have come. Come again, son. Don't forget a poor woman. My son would have been just like you—also fair,"—and stopped abruptly.

He was gazing at her as though he had been struck dumb with surprise, as though he had seen something from another world, and does not understand what is happening to him. Why is he responding so warmly to the words of this poor gypsy woman, to her voice, which had transformed her as she spoke, to her sincere glances that hid sadness and a deep warmth toward him....

He would have continued to sit there looking at her, who had so unwittingly warmed his heart, listening to her words so full of generosity and love, had she not changed the subject, and had his horse, tethered outside, not whinnied.

"Son, my handsome blue-eyed lad, would you like me to read your fortune before you leave me?" she asked entreatingly, and, without waiting for his reply, out of a chest she pulled a pack of dirty cards, worn from constant use.

"Very well," he agrees reluctantly," tell me my fortune, but tell the truth, be it bad or good, because I have never yet had my fortune told. If you predict my fate truthfully, I'll invite you to my wedding, just as I have invited another like you—and you'll receive a good payment. So play your cards ... and prophesy!"

Mavra obeyed.

Mavra had foretold the future with her cards for many, but had never seen a future so complicated, so doomed as this young man's.

Here is what her cards tell her:

"My son," says Mavra almost devoutly, looking at him earnestly, "you have two souls. One is fair, like a lady, splendid and proud, who does not want to know everyone, and the other is like the wind, son, it does not abide by the earth, it is attached to nothing. It wanders and vacillates. Who are you, really, son? Whom do you take after? Who was fair—your father or mother?" Asking these questions, she looks at him more closely with her large, black, sad eyes. "Who are you son? A prince?" Unbeknownst to her, tears darken her gaze. "Tell me, lad. My son would have been like you...." She nearly groaned and stopped.

Hryts was shaken by her words, recalling that he was a foundling, that he knew nothing about his real parents. He remained silent, thinking: "Let her continue. Maybe she'll learn from the cards who my parents are," for his adoptive parents call him a tramp, and he knows nothing more.

So he does not reply to her questions.

"A fairy tale," he only said dryly, waving a hand disdainfully.

"Are you and your parents from around here," persists Mavra, "or from somewhere else ... from somewhere, son, where you yourself have never set foot? But what is this? There are two fathers here for you, and two mothers, but it also shows that you are an orphan. Who are you, son? Who divided you like this?" she asks again, her eyes fixed on the handsome young face, the blue eyes, the black moustache. "Who are you?"

He remains silent and she, too, falls silent. For some reason she was about to cry, her eyes were filling with tears.

She had never seen him before, had never met him, yet felt as if she knew him, sensed something dear and close about him.... And those eyes ... those eyes that she had seen somewhere before!

Where? She does not know.

But she had seen them during her life, she had. With all her shattered soul she sensed that she had seen them, had even looked into them, *felt* them on her. Oh, a long time ago, a long, long time ago, *his eyes!* Yes, *his eyes!* She almost cried out, but was silent. Hryts remained calm, almost resisting, so she kept quiet.

"Do not love dark eyes, son," she says at last in a stifled voice, lifting her finger in warning and with a frown on her face. "Because dark eyes and blue eyes do not make a pair—they bring grief, they rock the soul. Love those like your own, then your future will be bright. Or wait," she added suddenly, "who is this one who is in love with you? Beside her there is grief and a roadway. A long, wide roadway. And you with a wedding on your mind—you also seem to be preparing for a journey. A far, distant journey. *Can it be that you love two?*" she asked abruptly, coldly, looking at him searchingly. "Do not love two, son," she warns again, "you will cleave your fate in two." She paused, then: "Yes, be wary of girls, both fair and dark.... For your mother, son, I see orphanhood, sorrowful and painful orphanhood, like no other mother in the world has experienced. Sorrow covers everything, though you are standing close to her. Sorrow covers everything here. There is happiness for you, but...," she did not complete her sentence. "Enough for the first time. Go!" She ended somewhat sadly, gathering her cards together and standing up.

Hryts rose also, feeling as if he had returned from the other world. He pulled out a few coins and threw them arrogantly at the old woman's feet.

She does not look at the money, but bows humbly to him, with her arms crossed.

"I don't want your money, son," she says, "allow me something else. Permit me, a poor gypsy woman, to bless you. You probably won't come to see me again, but you are dear to me. My son would have been like you if he were alive. *Fair* he was. I bless you, my son, may happiness always be yours, like sunshine over the earth." Having said this and without waiting for his permission, she suddenly raised herself on her toes, grabbed his head and pressed it to her breast, then let him go. "Go, son, maybe we won't see each other again...."

"You must come to my wedding, nanny," he answered, deeply moved by her unexpected kindness and quickly left the house.

It is quiet in Mavra's house.

Who is this boy?

She knew everyone in the village down in the valley, so she knew he wasn't from her village. In her solitude she clasped her head in her hands. Lord, he was handsome, and yet ... somehow.... See how much money he left her. He must be a wealthy man's son. Yet she was left with a feeling of neither joy nor sadness, which tore at her breast, and finally drove her outdoors.

The rain had stopped. A mist was rising out of the valleys and ravines between the mountains, as well as the forests. Rising, they drift in grey clouds and spirals over the forests, between the crests of age-old firs, as though bidding them farewell, racing each other mournfully somewhere into the distance.

Mavra is melancholy.

Melancholy and sad.

A young man had come like the moonrise into her house, eliciting a deep sadness in her soul. Why is she melancholy? He is a stranger, someone else's child, she tells herself, and she is a poor gypsy. A woman all alone on the entire mountain, in the entire forest—alone, always alone. She is bound to no one, has no one, is needed by no one. Why is she melancholy now that he has gone? Will she ever see him again? He invited her to his wedding. Whom is he marrying? What village does he live in? She had not even thought to ask. She had become so distracted by looking at him that she had not asked. But she will find out. A sudden thought strikes her: perhaps he is Tetiana's Hryts?

But, no. Hryts has not yet sent matchmakers to Tetiana. At least, Tetiana has not mentioned it yet. Yet he looked the way the girl had described him to her. He also rode off on a black horse, but it is not Hryts. Come what may, even if he isn't Hryts she will go. Not for charity, but to see him once again. Those eyes ... those eyes ... that had drifted from somewhere into her solitude in the forest.

* * *

There is silence all around ... silence....

The forest stands silent, but the firs are whispering something. Yet a hum is sounding through the forest ... saying something.

* * *

Hryts rides swiftly down the mountain along the White Path. Any moment now he will see the valley between the trees, so he does not have far to go. His thoughts, however, linger on his meeting with the solitary old gypsy fortune-teller. He recalls his meeting with her again and again. His heart is heavy with pity for her, heavy and melancholy. Although she had never seen him before, she had immediately wound a warm silken fold around his heart. And although he did not believe in fortune-tellers, for all of them deceive, he believes her alone. What hurt him unconsciously more than anything else was her humility toward him. Why did she humble herself to him? She owed him nothing and was guilty of nothing before him. She had seen him for the first time and seemed to lay all the warmth of her soul at his feet.... Like that old man, Andronati, who had always been so good to him and always begged him not to forget him. One day he will tell the old man about the fortune-teller Mavra and ask him to visit her. It might be good for the two of them to meet.

"My handsome prince," the caressing, humble words ring in his memory. "My blue-eyed dove."

Never in all his life had his own mother talked to him like that, though she called herself his mother.

His mother? Bah! He remembered with a bitter smile. Who knows where and who his mother is. She abandoned him like a puppy under a stranger's roof, to get rid of him, leaving him to the good graces of strangers, and she had never returned. Is he not alone, too, in this world, like that poor woman said: in the entire forest, on the entire mountain? Does his fate not resemble hers? "Mavra!" His sad and melancholy young heart cried, consciously seeking love—the true, pure mother love that he had never fully known, no matter how his adoptive parents loved him, or the girls, or how his friends and companions, or everyone who knew him, respected him. Generous, warm, mother love had never been his. She was the first and only one who had spoken to him with maternal warmth. He sensed strongly the truth in her words and feelings toward him. He will never forget her....

While full of these thoughts about her, he kept recalling her prophesies about his fate.

"Do not love dark eyes, son," she had warned, raising her finger, "because dark eyes and blue eyes do not make a pair. Love those that are like your own and your future will be bright."

These words echoed loudly in his soul. "*Turkynia has dark eyes*," he said to himself. Yet in that moment he clearly realized, as perhaps never before, how dear those same dark eyes were to him, as well as the one who had those dark eyes. Turkynia! responded his melancholy heart, that was forgetting everything, yet remembering her. Turkynia, come!

Unbeknownst to him, tears filled his eyes and sadness engulfed him. He rides along the White Path through the forest, and reckons that he will probably never travel it again. He will soon be in the village. He hears the loud, rushing waters of the stream down in the ravine. Overflowing with the rain waters that were draining down the mountainside, it raged along, paying attention to nothing and no one. But he must hurry. The rain and the time he had spent with the gypsy had made him late. His horse trots briskly down the white, rain-washed path, now straight and even.

Here and there the lower branches of the firs catch at his hat, showering him with fresh drops of the recent rain.

Dusk is descending the mountain and into the thickness of the firs, through which the setting sun, appearing again after the storm, here and there flashes its dying rays.

So it is.

But who is this coming up the path toward him? Can it be Turkynia? It is—it is Turkynia!

He cries out joyfully:

"Tetiana, is that you?" But then he falls silent.

It is Tetiana. She recognizes him, but motions to him to be silent. She is not far from her home. He stops his horse, turning him off the path, while she runs toward him. Barefoot, with streaming hair, her skirt tucked up as if she had stolen out of the house carrying some small bundle in her hands, she stops beside him, laughing and radiant.

Who would have expected this meeting? They cried out with pleasure at this unexpected joy.

"Don't talk loudly," warns Tetiana, out of breath from this unanticipated joy. "Don't talk loudly because Mother is coming up behind me."

"Do you love me?" he asks before anything else, bending down from his horse toward her and she, lithe and tall as a fir, stands on tiptoes to reach him.

"I do," she answers with eyes full of joy. "When haven't I loved you?"

He pulls her longingly into his arms and holds her to him with tenderness and strength, as never before. Then kisses her....

"No one can see us here," he whispers passionately.

"Kiss me again!"

"Only once more," she kisses him obediently.

"No. Again," he demands, and kisses her again. "I'm in a hurry, my cuckoo, I'm always working. We'll meet in the *forest sometime, like now*" he added furtively like a thief in flight.

She smiled happily.

"Like now," she repeated without thinking, and waited.

"*We'll meet*," he said hurriedly and began to move.

"*We'll meet*," she answered, looking at him with her soul in her eyes. And following him with her eyes, she walked with her head turned back, up the White Path down which he was descending....

Slapping his horse and taking a quick look back at her, he dashed down the hill like the wind and disappeared from her sight.

The galloping horse stirred the fir branches, agitating the drops of rain that had settled on them. They fell thickly to the ground, trickling one after another, then slowing down, stopped altogether.

Silence then settled in the forest....

* * *

"Hey, on St. John's Eve, hey on Kupala.... Hey-hey-hey!" Tetiana's happy voice resounds unexpectedly somewhere on the mountainside and dies away.

"A beautiful maiden was seeking her fate, hey-hey-hey," finishes Ivanykha Dub in her heart, following her daughter slowly and with dignity up the mountain path to Mavra.

* * *

One day, perhaps three weeks after Tetiana's encounter with Hryts, Ivanykha Dub again sends Tetiana to Mavra. She wants to find out how she is, because she has not come down to the mill for some time. She also gives Tetiana a bundle of food for her.

Tetiana is eager to go, and preparing for the visit, she adorns her head with flowers. Perhaps today she will meet her darling whom she has not seen for so long. He has work, he said. It happened before that they had met unexpectedly on the White Path ... just like the last time.

She left, walking along thoughtfully.

Her thoughts are always with Hryts. How he will finally come to her home, how he will send the matchmakers, how her mother will plan the wedding, how they will live afterward, what happiness awaits them, success, and so on. Hryts will take over the mill and become a man of property. Everyone will love and respect him. Her mother can then retire and rest, living with them. Her good mother has always thought of her happiness, prayed for it, and now her prayers would be answered by handsome Hryts as her son-in-law. If she does not wish to stay with them, she will go into a nunnery, to which she has been drawn since her father's death. Or else she will live peacefully with them, in quiet happiness. Everything will be as she wishes. Whatever she desires, so it will be.

With these happy thoughts Tetiana makes her way, pausing from time to time as if to rest, then stopping suddenly to listen.

From the very start she senses footsteps following her lower down on the White Path, heavy and slow footsteps.

She stands listening and looking down—waiting.

Maybe it is Hryts?

No, it cannot be. He always rides his horse. It is almost as if they were inseparable—he and his horse. He has never met her without him. That horse alone shares their secret, the forest, too. No, it is not Hryts.

She waits another moment, then calls out anyway, as she always does:

"I'm here!"

The echo answers from the forest, "here!," dispersing the sound and dying away.

She starts up again.

After a little while she stops again for a moment. The firs on the left and the right seem to stop with her. Some along the ravine, others up the mountainside all seem to be waiting. Rocking their crests lightly, they rustle cautiously—as if listening with her, and hearing nothing, appear to be whispering to each other....

"Hryts!"

"Is that you, Hryts?" she calls out again. "I'm here!"

Automatically she lifts her hand to the red poppies adorning her head, making sure they are in place, because this is the way he likes her.

No, it isn't Hryts.

Following her out of the depths of the forest comes the old grey-haired figure of some terrifying, ancient gypsy, who is moving slowly toward her like a shadow.

Tetiana became frightened. She had never seen this old man in the village where she knows all the poor very well, often seeing them at her charitable mother's home. But here he was, folding his hands devoutly and bowing to her, as she had seen only Mavra doing, when someone had given her something and she was respectfully thanking them. She is afraid of him, but tried not to show it, for she was not easily frightened. He perceives this, however, and again bows humbly before her.

"Don't be frightened, daughter, of an old man" he says. "He is lost in the forest, but is going far and means no harm to anyone. How good that I have met you here," he continues, his dark eyes sweeping over her with covert ill-will.

"Why should I be frightened?" asks Tetiana, stepping aside to let the old man pass her easily on the path. Then quickly she takes something out of Mavra's bag and gives it to him. "Accept this, good father, for the souls of the dead," she says humbly, "and tell me, if you would be so kind, where you are coming from? From some great distance, perhaps? Are you going far?"

"No, my good child. I have just come from the valley today, from your village," answers the old gypsy, continuing to look closely at the young girl with her red poppies, who had appeared like a nymph before him.

"And were you able to get many alms in our village?" asks Tetiana, smiling timidly and hoping with all her heart to get away from the old man as quickly and as far away as possible.

"Enough. Thanks to all the good people who help the poor. They treated me *well*. I did not turn to them *in vain*, and what I wished to *find out*—I did. This is the third time I have come to this village. I'm more often in Tretivka. The first time I was here was more than twenty years ago, a time I don't wish to recall; I passed through a second time during the winter, now this is the third and probably the last time. I don't know how fate will treat me. But I had to come. I have taken upon myself a task to help someone—so I came. But who knows if I will come again."

"Why?" asks the girl trustingly.

"My age will not permit me. And who would want to look after an old gypsy?" The old man leaned pensively on his cane. Leaning thus, he continues to look at the girl out of the corner of his eye. The girl senses his gaze and again feels fear. At last he asks:

"Would you tell me, daughter, who you are? So beautiful, so stately, so charming."

"I am the daughter of a widow," answers Tetiana modestly and with dignity.

"A wi-dow?" as if in wonder.

"A widow."

"Aha!" says the old man and again stares at her red flowers, the golden half-moons hanging from her ears, swaying lightly with every movement of her head.

"Ah," he begins again, drawling his words, "if you are a widow's daughter, perhaps you could do something for me, so I can then return to my village. They are waiting for me there and I'm in a hurry."

"Why not?" Tetiana agrees gravely, happy in the hope that she will soon be rid of the old gypsy, and arching her expressive eyebrows, as she always does when surprised. She still cannot rid herself of some unexplained fear of the old man.

"Then tell me first," he begins, "whether you know the mill-owner Ivanykha Dub, a devout gentlewoman who is charitable to the poor?"

"Yes, I do, Grandpa, I do," Tetiana answers merrily and trustingly.

"In whose home is an only daughter, proud and spoiled, the prettiest girl in the village."

Tetiana flushed.

"Yes, I do, Grandpa, yes," she answers, trying to ignore his sharp glances and laughing. "I know them both. But what do you want from them, from Ivanykha Dub?"

"Nothing from the mother, child. My business is with the young one, the beautiful sorceress who leads young men astray and who, they say, bewitches with her dark brows, her red flowers, and conquers with her eyes."

Tetiana began to laugh heartily.

"They call her Turkynia."

"Turkynia, Grandpa," repeated the girl, who was becoming graver by the minute and wishing to get away from the old man. "What is your business with Turkynia, Grandpa? Tell me quickly," she urges him, "because I have to hurry. I am on my way to visit a poor woman, I am taking her some food, and she is expecting me."

"To a poor woman?" asks the gypsy, looking at her unbelievingly, and especially at her red flowers.

"To a poor woman."

"Then may the Blessed Virgin bless you for your kind heart. You've already given to one and are carrying gifts to another. You are very kind and generous. And who are you, daughter, so that I may remember you?" he asks again without taking his eyes off her.

"This is foolishness," answers Tetiana impatiently, "Better say what you want from Turkynia who, as they say, leads young men astray."

The old man sighs, straightens up, and, as if seeing something unusual above the girl's head, begins:

"Child, it is hard to wound another's heart, and since I have already been asked, since it is necessary, since someone wishes it, then I'll pass a message along."

"Who asked?" inquires Tetiana, trembling in anticipation and fear at hearing something unpleasant.

"Blue-eyed Nastia."

"I don't know her," says Tetiana, her eyebrows arched.

"Nastia, from Tretivka, who will be getting married."

"To whom?" Her eyes widen with expectation.

"Right away, daughter, just don't interrupt."

"And what does blue-eyed Nastia want from Turkynia?"

"She asked thus," begins the old man. "Stand, she said, before Turkynia and say this:

'Turkynia, I have heard that you love Hryts, the finest lad on the Hungarian border. That you enticed him with flowers and words, that you cause misery, take away happiness.

'And I have heard, Turkynia, that Hryts does not love you, because for a long time now he has been caressing another. He has chosen blue-eyed Nastia for his own and will soon be marrying her.

'What do you want of him, beautiful Turkynia? That he should abandon his first love and marry you? You would then be cursed not only by her, but by all the people who will hear about it. Laughter and derision will follow you through the village and you will be left in grief, a shadow of yourself.

'And I have heard, Turkynia, that you are wealthy, that you can easily find another, without Hryts. You should know that Hryts's young bride-to-be cries because of you, sorrows because of you, curses you bitterly. He loved her long before he saw you; caressed you while wooing her. That is why he will take her before he will send matchmakers to woo you.

'Turkynia, I have heard all this that I am telling you from the fair Nastia, whom Hryts is marrying. He himself complained to her that you are to blame for this distress, that you bewitched him, turned his head.

'With your dark brows you adorned yourself and at the same time divided his soul. You wandered the forest, played at echoes, leading him astray....

'Now he has come to his senses. He is rejecting you, he is afraid of your dark brows, he loves lighter ones. He will not meet you any more, so do not wait, unless perchance you see him on his black horse. Then turn away, so people will not know that you loved Hryts, that you were taking him away from another.

'If you won't stop approaching him, then you should know that people will not be silent. Disgrace will follow the dark-browed one who separated Hryts from Nastia for all time, took away his heart, divided his soul—with your evil spirit drove him to despair.... Yes.'

"I, an old man, have witnessed it all. Tell that to Turkynia, child, if you know her well. Tell her that Hryts has another. He is inviting people to his wedding and I will be there, too." The old gypsy ended with these words, and waited.

Tetiana slipped down to his feet.

"I am Turkynia, Grandpa" she cried, clasping his knees, then almost unconscious, said no more.

The old man shuddered.

"Really, truly, you? Why didn't you tell me right away that you were Tetiana Dub, then maybe I would not have told you everything. I thought you might be Ivanykha's daughter, but I wasn't sure, although those who know you described you very well. I even found you here, where they said I would. You are beautiful, Turkynia—they weren't lying. I have paid you meanly for the alms you gave me, but I am not to blame. I knew nothing about it. Nastia told me and he told Nastia. He loves both of you, but he is marrying her. You should not have started this with Hryts, neither with your dark brows, your red flowers, nor your sweet words.... No.... I don't know what else you charmed him with. I cannot be blamed for this. You yourself know that you have caused distress. That was why I was asked to tell you all this. For once, let Hryts have peace!"

"No, Grandpa," Tetiana spoke up at last, turning her pale, benumbed face up to the old man, still clasping his knees tightly in her grief. "No, Grandpa, I didn't start anything, I did no evil. I just loved Hryts.... Oh, no," she nearly groans, "it cannot be that he is taking another. It cannot be!" She almost screamed and again bowed her head against his knees, clasping them tightly in desperation.

The old man shrugged.

"I don't know, daughter," he said dryly, "that's what I was told. I am not from these parts. What I knew I have told you. I had to.")

"Oh-h-h!" groaned Tetiana, wounded to the heart, still kneeling and pressing her face to the old man's knees. "Oh-h-h!"

"Yes, daughter," confirmed the old man, "all that the *blue-eyed Nastia* told me is true. Hryts himself has invited me to the wedding and I intend to be there."

"No, Grandpa," cries Tetiana, as she had earlier, in a frantic though confident voice, still embracing the old man's knees in inexpressible and humble grief, as though she cannot make any other movement, and praying as though a saint were before her. "No, Grandpa, don't say that. It *cannot be....* We met in the forest ... just a few days ago," she sobbed, "a few days ago." With these words she subsided as if extinguished. Then: "And he ... he even kissed. This *cannot be*, it isn't true; he is not marrying another.... He loves me. I didn't start this," she cried. "I only loved, Grandpa, I only *loved! We are promised to one another* and he said that before the snow falls I would be in his house! He loves me. Here ... here ... in the forest ... how many times ... in the *forest....*" And again she seems to swoon.

The old man laughed heartily.

"You say he loves you?"

Tetiana looked up to him in appeal, then dropped her head again in despair.

"He does, good Grandfather, he loves me," she said earnestly, again pressing her head against the old man's knees. "He loves only me, *only me in the whole world.* He told me this himself and I believe him. Before the snow falls, he said, you'll be in my house. I am *his* Turkynia!" she cried, falling face down to the ground.

The old man lifted her up.

"You won't be, Turkynia," he declared firmly. "The blue-eyed Nastia will be in it and Hryts, I assure you, is inviting people to the wedding. He has already asked me. I will be there. Get up, come to your senses. Don't think about Hryts, don't cloud his happiness, beware of sin—or else, you'll see!" With these words he shook his fist at her threateningly, as if submitting to some command. Tetiana gaped at him with distracted, wide-open eyes, but finally comprehending his words and threatening gesture, like a serpent rose from the ground and stood up.

"*You* go away!" She shouted in a savage voice, boiling over with sudden hatred, as if in his final words all the filth in the world lay before her. "*You,* go!" She shoved the old man from her so vigorously that he fell. "*You,* go, you are an evil spirit who has found me. Hryts!" She called out with all her strength and despair, then laughing wildly, shouted, "Hryts, I'm here!"

The old man's gypsy eyes gleamed angrily as he picked himself up and threatened her again with his fist and stick.

"Just you wait, just you wait," he shouted, panting and cursing horribly. "So this is what a sorceress-witch is like, she thinks that only she is right. Now I see for myself that Nastia was telling the truth. I'm telling you from her and again from me that Hryts is marrying her and *leaving you.*"

"Not true! He loves me!" She threw herself at him wildly, her eyes equally wild, defending herself with all her strength against the old man's terrible words.

"That's all you're going to get!" the old man cried out, laughing bitterly. "That's all. Just like his father who once loved his mother," he added with equally bitter hatred in his voice. *"That's all you're going to get!"*

Tetiana, not understanding what he was saying except for his last words, threw herself at him again.

"Go away!" she shouted and arching her dark brows she pointed an arm toward the nearby ravine. "Go" she repeated, "throw yourself into it and never come back!"

The old man looked at her in terror, and bending over to pick up his stick that had fallen to the ground, wanted to hit her with it.

But she was gone—she had disappeared. Only from the direction in which she had taken flight did he hear a loud, despairing cry: *"Hryts!... I'm here,"* followed by long, hysterical laughter.

*   *   *

Out of breath, her face haggard and pale, her lips contorted, and with a lost look in her eyes, Tetiana bursts in on her mother and throws herself against her breast.

"Mother!" she exclaimed in a strange, stifled voice, "Mother, Hryts has abandoned me. I've been betrayed. He loved me, but is marrying another. Mother!" Without giving her mother time to take in her words, she shakes her unconsciously with all her strength. "Mother! He was loving *two of us at the same time.* Listen, *Mother!"*

Ivanykha Dub, had been sitting on a bench, and suddenly seeing her half-mad daughter before her, could do nothing but brace herself against the wall.

"What Hryts?"

"The one who was once here last winter riding a horse. So handsome! We used to meet in the forest. We loved each other there. Only the forest knew it. *Hryts*, Mother!" She laughed wildly.

Ivanykha Dub rose heavily to her feet.

"Yes?" said her mother, and added: "He told *you* to seek the fern blossom?" and smiled as if for the last time in her life.

"Mother!" She cried out hopelessly for the whole house to hear, "Mother!"

"You were my *one* and only," said her mother, "my *one* and only in the whole world."

"Mother!"

Ivanykha Dub did not answer.

Tetiana fell on her knees before her and confessed.

* * *

An hour later Tetiana is in the forest again.

With frenzied steps she flies like an arrow to old Mavra. "Mavra!" her voice seems to pound in her breast with a savage groan, seeking release. "Mavra!" until finally she arrived.

The old gypsy was alarmed at the girl's appearance and embraced her at once.

"Daughter," she says, "child, what has happened?"

"Mavra!" was all she heard from the dead weight against her chest.

The old woman's eyes filled with a presentiment of calamity.

"He?" she merely asked, her voice filled with indescribable grief.

"He is marrying another. He has betrayed me," wailed Tetiana.

"You see? And you thought that he would always love you, my child."

"Oh Mavra! He loved and caressed me, he kissed me, made promises. Just days ago in the forest, Mavra, and now...."

Mavra suddenly began to laugh as if at a child.

"So-o-o," she drawled out spitefully, "caressed and kissed?"

"Caressed, kissed ... the last time when he was on his horse, after the storm. And oh ... so tenderly...."

"After the storm?" the old woman says, surprised. "It was *he*?" She shakes her head sorrowfully, recalling the day, and whispers: "Lord, Lord." Then she said firmly and with hatred:

"You should know, daughter, that he who professes the greatest love betrays the quickest. His heart is already saying farewell while he is kissing you. Who among them *has not done this?*"

"Oh-h-h, Mavra!" Tetiana raised her arms above her head in despair. "I will go mad!"

"No, daughter you won't go mad," Mavra consoled her. "I didn't go mad either. Just think," she said calmly, "not only he, but everyone rejected me, cast me into the forest like an animal, out of their midst, they took my child. You won't go mad. I am still alive today, without going mad, I am alone in the world, on this mountain, in this forest, and all because of love's caresses. And I didn't go mad. Ha-i, ha-i," she ended with her habitual sing-song, shaking her head, "you won't go mad."

And surely you did [handwritten marginalia]

"But *I* will go mad, Mavra," insisted the girl dully. "*I* will go mad. I can't endure it. What shall I do, Mavra?"

Mavra shrugs her shoulders helplessly, but after thinking a moment or two, says:

"I'll go see him and ask him myself. I'll find out if that's the truth. Who told you all this? Where did you find this out?

"Some old gypsy whom I met on my way to you. In the forest. He told me everything. He wasn't lying." Here she told Mavra about her meeting with old Andronati.

"How did he know?" Mavra asked with unusual curiosity.

"Hryts's bride-to-be herself told him to convey the message to me."

The old gypsy cursed, but calmed down after a moment and said:

"Hush, child, hush. I'll go there myself, I'll find out, and bring back the truth. Hush, and don't worry. But you may be sure that if this is the truth, they'll never know happiness, neither he, nor she. I'm like a mother to you—and where a mother curses, there is no happiness."

Tetiana was silent, immobile.

"I'll try to turn him back to you," Mavra promised in a soothing voice.

At these words Tetiana reacted as though bitten by a venomous snake. She pushed Mavra away from her with the same surprising display of pride and arrogance she had shown Andronati earlier, so that the old woman fell on the bench.

"Don't you dare!" she cried, drawing herself up in all her youthful slenderness, her brows arched. "*I* did not betray, I did not love two. Don't you dare! I loved him faithfully," she said, her lips drained of color, "him *alone*. He betrayed me, so what is there to *turn back*? Don't you dare!"

"Then this is what you get for your faithfulness," retorted Mavra, offended, in an exasperated voice.

"Yes, that's what I got," said Tetiana, breathing heavily in her agitation, and was silent.

"He will get married and become the biggest landowner in the whole village—and you?"

Tetiana did not reply, only turned paler.

"He will get married and become the biggest landowner in the whole village—and you?" repeated Mavra, now irritated.

Tetiana glanced at Mavra. Dear God, what eyes! What an expression they held, and with this look she was begging and pleading. Then she answered:

"I will be *Tetiana*, who else should I be?"

Mavra did not understand.

"And what will you do to him?"

"What did *you* do, Mavra?" Tetiana almost hissed the question. Mavra did not reply, then cursing, finally she answered:

"I accepted my fate, submitted to it, and I have lived with it to this very day. What else could I do?"

Tetiana looked at her unseeingly.

"*You*, Mavra," she said, "you submitted. You were able to do it."

"And what will you do, child? He won't marry you now."

"He won't marry me. He will *never* marry me," answered the girl, distractedly.

"You've lost your happiness ... your future," began Mavra, and shook her head sorrowfully, according to her habit.

"You don't say!" the girl answered abruptly, and glancing at Mavra with burning eyes, she quickly left the house.

After reflecting for a moment, Mavra ran after her:

"Come again in two days," she called. "I'll go and enquire tomorrow and come back with the truth. Come again, I say...."

Tetiana looked around, but did not reply. She walked swiftly with uneven strides along the White Path, down into the valley, and disappeared from the old woman's sight.

* * *

Turning back into the house, Mavra thumped her head with her fist.

"So that was Hryts, my prince! He who would ride a black horse, just as Tetiana said, for he was here with him. He is from Tretivka, on the other side of Chabanytsia. Oh God, where was my head when he was here? I told him his fortune and did not guess that it was Tetiana's Hryts! Where was my head? They cooed in the forest like birds, maybe even close by, and I didn't take heed. Tetiana, dear heart, what will happen to you now? I can see that you are not Mavra, you cannot endure pain, your grief has already overpowered you. God, be merciful! You've had everything you've wanted since childhood, everything you ever wished for. It was always as you wanted.... And now...." Mavra clasped her head in her hands, but soon recovered her self-control. She will go to him. Tomorrow. As soon as it grows light she will be at his home. She knows everything now. She'll fall at his feet and beg him from the bottom of her heart. "Son, my handsome prince, I'll entreat him, do not destroy Tetiana. *I* nursed her from childhood,

I took care of her, loved her. What is it that you don't like about her? Her height, her dark brows, her devotion? My son, don't destroy her!")

Maybe he will listen.

Nope

* * *

Tetiana passed two days and two nights, barely lying down to sleep. She neither ate nor drank, just waited, walked about as if half-asleep, saw nothing, heard nothing, and was always on the White Path in the forest. She would pause a moment at the spot where he had caressed her, or look about where he had usually waited for her, then call out "I'm here!" She was constantly and fever-ishly on the move, until she lost strength and a marked change came over her.

Her mother understands and does not try to stop her. She knows that peace is necessary for a stricken soul. Let her first overcome her grief alone. And then there is God.

The forest is good for her.

There is a church-like peace in the forest. Peace and God. She has grown up in it, and she will lose her pain in it. Her mother merely keeps watch and guards her like a shadow, so that she will not do herself any harm. Guarding her, she also prays: "God, let her come to no harm, give her strength, lead her to peace." Ivanykha Dub has also changed, she is not herself. Within a short, sorrowful period her hair has turned white. She seems to have bent with age, awaiting death....

Returning from the forest on the third day, Tetiana told her mother:

"I'm going up to Mavra. I need Mavra. I'll come back, I'll be back soon."

Her mother embraced her silently. She sees that the girl is feverish, that her eyes stare blindly as if seeking something, that her body trembles.

"Go with God, my child, to Mavra, and God grant you a safe return," said the poor woman, fearing to let her leave her embrace. But the girl, who seemed to have been waiting for her mother's final words, tore herself from her arms and rushed in frenzied haste into the forest.

"God, let her come to no harm, give her strength, save her from death," the mother whispered as she went back into the house.

Tetiana now stands on the threshold of Mavra's house.

"Is it true, Mavra?" were her first words, spoken in a strange voice that sounded as if all the strings that had been playing until this time were now broken.

"It is true, daughter, true," says Mavra and in her soul she marvelled at the terrible change that had come over the girl. "I myself talked to Hryts. He's the one that was here in my home a while ago. As I've already said, I myself talked to him," and saying this her eyes never left the girl. "Daughter, he laughed at the fact that it was I who was assailing him on your behalf. 'A boy can love two at the same time,' he said, and that he loves you, Tetiana. Who would not love her? For her dark brows, her generous heart. He has never loved anyone as truly as he loved Turkynia. But it so happens that she is second in line—so she has to step aside. For although he loves both, he can't marry both, and even if he wanted to, the priest won't allow it. What does Tetiana want from him? How can he help her? By leaving Nastia? But Nastia will not step aside. He is afraid to leave Nastia. It is easier for Tetiana. She is rich, she'll get another, and everything will turn out well. He isn't worried about her. It is worse for him. Her dark-browed face is always before him, even though his wedding is but a week away. He will just have to suffer until he forgets her. The girls themselves are to blame, falling in love with him—and are now blaming him for it. It is bad enough that Nastia is angry, and here is Tetiana, also lamenting. What can he do about this misfortune? If he knew he would solve it, but he has no idea what to do about it. Let her, Mavra, tell Turkynia that he and Nastia will be married within a week, but that he loves her...."

After recounting this tale, Mavra was nearly in tears. "Oh," she cried, "I feel sorry for your Hryts, my child. Sorry for some reason, yet bitter, too. I am sorry for you because you are *mine*, and sorry for him, because somehow he is *mine*, too. Good God, why did it have to happen this way? He is so handsome, and you are so good, and it has all turned out so falsely. Just as it happened to me long ago. God forgive me, at least I sinned, betrayed my husband, but you...." And she stopped.

Tetiana did not reply.

She stood, pale and still as death in the doorway, her eyes roving about the room as if seeking something, her breathing laboured. When Mavra, taking pity on her, said: "You've lost your happiness, daughter, you've lost your future," she did not reply with a single word, but turned and fled from the house, as she had done earlier from her mother.

She runs along the White Path, staggering, trying to conquer her distress, but failing. She is overcome by it—it is stifling her. She only senses that something must happen—either to her or to *him*—she does not know which one. Something powerful, something immense, something that has never happened before must *happen* now that will kill the *evil* that has destroyed her happiness. The evil that is so immense, so cruel. God! Something is raging in her completely overwrought mind. Why is it here? Why is it so strong? Her first thought that something must *happen* reappears. The evil that has destroyed her happiness must be *destroyed. She* will kill it. She feels that she will kill it. That she is capable. But how? What?... She knows nothing.... Suddenly her mind becomes muddled. Who is to blame, she asks herself, Hryts? No, Hryts is not to blame. He loves her, he even told Mavra that he loves her. Is *Nastia* to blame? No, Nastia is not to blame. She has no happiness either. Hryts does not love her as he does Tetiana. She stops suddenly—but what if he does? Oh, he does, he does! Something shrieked with a bloody cry within her soul, conquering all her earlier thoughts. He loves her, otherwise he wouldn't be marrying her. He *loves* her! And then, with a terrible, insane mirth, she began to laugh uncontrollably.

Then she casts her mind back to her first thought. Is Hryts to blame? No, Hryts is not to blame. Her heart tells her that he isn't. *It is something else.* It is that evil something that has hidden itself within him and is stopping him which is to blame. *Evil!* It is to blame and must be destroyed. She will kill it. She.... She stopped suddenly as if thunderstruck, her hands behind her head, her eyes looking wildly about the forest, at the tops of the trees.... Who can tell her how she can get at this evil, the thought flashed through her mind. Who can tell her? No one. Because no one knows, only she is conscious of its existence. Something within her speaks suddenly. That's it! The fern blossom will tell her. The fern blossom! She will seek the fern blossom and it alone will tell her. And no one else will know or hear. It will tell her. Whoever finds the fern blossom, Hryts once told her, will know all there is to know in the world and will find happiness. So then, she will know. She will know how to approach this evil, how to destroy it. She will destroy it, her brain throbs, so that there will be no more of it in any corner of the world. Neither in her, nor in Hryts, nor in Nastia. It will not be anywhere. Then all will be well. But quickly, quickly ... she must do it quickly, or else she will be too late ... and she turned where she stood and rushed into the depths of the forest....

* * *

Tetiana had left Mavra's cottage without a word or a glance. Mavra was greatly troubled by this silence. What is keeping her lips closed? she asked herself, and she worried about the girl. Just in this short period of time

Tetiana had lost weight, grown pale, her eyes burned with a strange fire, and then.... What will happen *next*? God help her, she should not be allowed to become seriously ill. Or else ... or else ... even worse ... it was terrifying to think of it ... go out of her mind. It happens.

Tetiana had never known hardship or sorrow with her mother; she had had everything she ever wanted since childhood. This was the first time in her life that thunder had struck her. Her own tragic fate was being repeated with this child whom she had brought up and loved with all her heart. In this sheltered spot between the mountains, in this quiet forest, her personal tragedy was being repeated. Where had this misfortune come from? Who had caused it? The boy himself has become very dear to her. When she laid eyes on him, she saw the one from the Hungarian plain, because of whom her life had come to ruin. The only difference between her destiny and Tetiana's was that hers had happened on the Hungarian plain, and Tetiana's here, in the forest....

Mavra could no longer endure her thoughts of the past and Tetiana's misfortune in the tiny confines of her cottage and went outdoors.

It was a beautiful, warm, quiet evening.

The sky was brilliant with stars, and Mavra, sitting on the threshold of her cottage, gazed up at the moon. It was a full moon, appearing directly in front of her, over the forest-covered wall of the facing mountain and the ravine with its frothing river; it seemed to have stopped deliberately before her cottage.

Deep silence reigns, full of hallowed secrets in which everything around had become silently engulfed. Mavra sits with her eyes fixed as if praying to the moon that hangs glowing and unmoving over the mountain. All around her stand the dark, forest-covered mountains that beneath the light of the moon seem to touch the sky's horizon on every side and blend into it.

Mavra is praying to the moon, drowning her soul in it, and in Tetiana's misery. First Tetiana, then Hryts appear before her, they torment her, and lacerate her soul. Her heart aches at the thought of the terrible misery of the poor, betrayed girl who, knowing no evil, had never committed it herself—and now seems to have fallen from the heavens into an abyss. All this because of him. On the other hand, part of her speaks up in sympathy for Hryts. He is an orphan, so he had told her, without mother or father—a foundling—a foster-child. Where is he from, who are his parents? He did not know. He had been found on the threshold of the landowners' home wrapped in rags, believed to be gypsy rags, as his foster mother used to upbraid him.

In recalling his words Mavra felt as though her blood was afire. Her child had disappeared from her side, and three villages from here a child had been found on the doorstep of a wealthy landowner's home dressed in "gypsy rags."

"Oh Lord!" She sighs heavily and raises her arms in mute appeal, almost demented by the thought that perhaps ... perhaps ... *perhaps*—with an inward scream—*this is her son!* He is so like her lover from the Hungarian plain, and her son was *white*, Lord, *white!* But no, it cannot be. She is alone in her solitude and in her grief for Tetiana has gone completely mad, taking leave of her senses. At the thought of Tetiana her heart lurched painfully. Tetiana has been destroyed by him, destroyed.

But is he to blame?

Sometimes, he had told her, justifying himself about Tetiana—sometimes his heart was so drawn to other places, into the distance, to the ends of the earth, that he would have followed it without stopping. Seeking the cause, he would mount his horse and gallop away from home, just to get away, to seek change. In one such melancholy hour, whether good or evil, he had met Tetiana in the forest and fallen deeply in love with her. He was mad about her. He sees her before him day and night—her eyes, her dark brows, the flowers she wore; hears her laughter and loses his mind. He would have stolen her from her home like a thief and run off into the world forever if she, too, had not fallen in love with him. When she did, they met in the forest and were happy. But he must marry Nastia. That's what he is like. Even if faced with death he would be that way. What can you do with him?

"But Mother," he had told her, "you yourself warned me with your cards not to love dark eyes, because, you said, 'Dark eyes and blue do not make a pair. Take those that are like yours, then your future will be bright.'" Yet things are not happening as planned. He must marry Nastia. Only Nastia keeps him together body and soul, loves and forgives him, no matter what he does. She is always good to him. This is why she is his intended. He will not leave her. Tetiana is her mother's only child, has never known grief, she will cry a bit, grieve a little, and when all this is over ... she will marry another. He is not worried about her, although he is sorry for the beautiful Turkynia who will always remain in his heart. But what of it? She is not destined for him....

So he told her when she went to see him—this, and other things.

Looking now at the mountains and the sky thick with stars and a full moon, Mavra smiled bitterly. Just as no one had pitied her, Mavra—neither *he*, nor her husband nor her parents—so now her poor Tetiana is not pitied by *this one*. There's love for you!...

Thinking thus, Mavra almost dissolved into tears. The Lord only knows how the poor girl will endure her grief. And her mother? All her life she has prayed for her daughter's happiness, has concerned herself with the welfare of people—she saved her, Mavra, from hunger and death. The two of them—like one mother—trembled over the girl, guarded her, and in the end were unable to save her from tragedy and grief. She left her today like a wounded bird, without saying a word. What was she thinking? What was overflowing her heart? She seems to have forgotten how to talk—so transformed was she by her grief.

With these thoughts running through her mind old Mavra can think of nothing, one way or another, that will help Tetiana. She could give Hryts lovage or belladonna to turn him back to the girl, but Tetiana had attacked her when she mentioned it. She had gone completely mad. One moment she was speaking normally and the next as if she were taking leave of her senses. She is sorry for Hryts, too.... She doesn't know Nastia, the girl he is marrying, but she knows Tetiana. Her Tetiana! Why is she not the one fated to become his wife? In what way has he failed to unite with her in happiness? To love her to the utmost? To the utmost! With his beauty? He was beautiful like the moon in the heavens. In what other way? She does not know, but senses something here that is beyond her comprehension, that there is some tangle that she cannot unravel, that is overpowering and unclear to her. Nevertheless, she is still sorry for Hryts, although she is a stranger to him, a poor gypsy woman whom he might never again recall for the rest of his life. For some reason she is sorry for him and cannot bear him ill will. Her heart will not let her.

* * *

It was near midnight, but Mavra continued to sit, lost in thought.

She could not sleep.

Drowning in melancholy, she prayed to the moon and the stars. Has anyone else ever spent a night of such sadness, alone in the depths of the forest, as she has? she asked herself.

No—not really alone!

She is surrounded by the primeval forest, the moon before her and a rushing river in the abyss below, rushing and roaring in the sacred silence of the night, its waters glittering under the magic light of the moon and the stars above....

Not alone.

"Oh Lord, have mercy on us, forgive us our sins," she whispered, beating her breast, then stood up and went into the house.

* * *

The bedroom in Ivanykha Dub's house is faintly illuminated. A candle burns before the icon of the Blessed Virgin Mary, wavering and blinking. Ivanykha Dub is lying on the bed half-dressed, listening to Tetiana, lying not far from her, restlessly turning from side to side … from time to time murmuring something incomprehensible.

"You're not sleeping, child?" she finally asks, although she herself has not once closed her eyes. Under the constant strain of her daughter's grief, she watches her every move.

"No," answers Tetiana, springing suddenly from her bed. "What is making that rushing sound?"

"It's the river, dear."

"The river?"

"Yes. The river on which our mill and house stand. But sleep, dear, go to sleep. God is always with you. He always watches over you, and you are your mother's one and only in this world. Sleep...."

"I'm going, mother," Tetiana answers quickly, standing beside her mother's bed and looking at her with strange, feverish eyes, "I'm going out."

The mother, frightened, turns faint with distress and fear.

"Where, my precious?" she asks in a half-whisper, taking her daughter's hand carefully in her hands.

"To look for the fern blossom," says her daughter. "I'll know everything, Hryts told me—everything. So I'm going, mother."

In her terror the mother sees only her daughter's two dark eyes in the pale, haggard face.

"Don't go out now, it's night, dear," she urges her softly, holding back her tears. "It's midnight. You'll go tomorrow. If you go now, you'll be leaving me all alone."

"Tomorrow isn't midnight," says Tetiana, and then, seeming to come to her senses, sits down obediently near her mother.

"Tomorrow isn't midnight, daughter. Tomorrow is Sunday."

"Sunday. Yes, yes, Sunday," Tetiana catches on to her mother's words and adds quietly: "Mavra said: '*On Sunday morning...*,'" and she broke off suddenly, as though remembering something else. After a moment she began again: "On Sunday morning...."

"On Sunday morning," says her mother quickly, "you'll go on Sunday morning. We'll both go and pray to God."

"To look for the blossom," says Tetiana as if awakening and looking about the room dully.

"To look for the blossom," her mother repeats softly, embracing her sick daughter, her eyes filling with tears. "Hush, precious, hush. Sleep, my dear, sleep!" She soothes the girl, stroking and caressing her like a small child.

"I'll know everything then," murmurs Tetiana in a sing-song voice, cuddling up to her mother trustingly, and closing her eyes as if to sleep. "I'll know ev-ery-thing."

"You'll know everything," her mother also murmurs.

"And when the *snow falls I'll be in your house*," Tetiana speaks up again.

"You'll be in my house," whispers her mother cautiously, realizing instinctively that her daughter is talking to Hryts.

"I'll co-ome!" Tetiana suddenly cries out in a choked tone, hiding her head against her mother's breast.

"Come, my cuckoo, come," whispers her mother, holding her breath so as not to disturb Tetiana's madness with any movement. "Come!"

"*I am Turkynia....*"

"My beautiful Turkynia."

"Your one and only in the whole world...."

"*My one and only in the whole world....*"

"Yours," whispers Tetiana, like a sleepy child.

"Mine...."

Quiet descended.

Tetiana breathes fitfully while heavy, hot tears slide down her mother's face....

"Yours," murmurs Tetiana under her breath.

"Mine."

At last there was silence.

* * *

Ivanykha Dub sits immobile, looking at the pale face of her unhappy child, as though at an angel's image, who wakes up every few minutes, drifting in and out of delirium.

After a few interminable moments of silence, she seems to quiet down.
Ivanykha Dub bends over her, weeping and trembling with anxiety.

Is Tetiana sleeping? She is now so quiet ... quiet....

Yes, it seems that she is sleeping.

But no.

She is not asleep. She raises her head from her mother's bosom, opens her
eyes wide and asks again:

"What is that rushing sound, mother?"

"It is the river."

"The river?"

"Yes, my daughter. The river on which our mill and house stand."

Tetiana then closes her eyes again and cuddling up to her mother tenderly
and trustfully, she smiles and begins to sing softly:

> "Hey, on St. John's Eve, hey on Kupala's Eve, Hey, hey, hey!...
> A beautiful maiden her fortune sought—hey, hey, hey!...

"Hey, hey, hey," repeats her mother, trying to stem the flow of tears, "hey,
hey, hey!..."

"Her fortune sought," murmurs Tetiana for the last time, and falls asleep.

"Her fortune sought," repeats her mother in a faint whisper.

* * *

On Sunday morning Tetiana rushes out of the house into the forest.

Her mother does not stop her, seeing that it only leads to worse when she
tries. Let her leave her grief behind in the forest, she thinks, let her have
some liberty for a time and freedom in everything she desires, then we'll
see....

Here in the valley she is unable to calm her, so let her be as her heart
desires. The stillness of the forest will heal her soul. Every succeeding day
will calm her. And then.... Perhaps old Mavra will help to cheer her up,
she is like a second mother to her. In the meantime she, her mother, is
helpless.

* * *

With a strange gait Tetiana strides up and down the slopes of the White Path, at times with her eyes wide open, then half-closed, as though she were dreaming, her thoughts always on the evil that must be destroyed, until she finds herself near Mavra's house.

But why is she going to Mavra's. She did not plan on coming here. She has come out to look for the fern blossom. Ah, she suddenly remembers, she wanted Mavra to ask about Hryts and to give her some advice on how to deal with this evil. Mavra? She begins to laugh. Mavra will be of no help. She will not go to Mavra—Mavra frightens her now. Mavra does not love her any more. She loves Nastia.

In her despair she did not notice that she had reached Mavra's open window.

Yes, she is afraid of Mavra, but now that she is here, she will hide herself beneath her window. With this half-mad thought she sinks on the bank against the wall below Mavra's window. Burying her hands in her hair which has already become dishevelled and hangs in a dark, silken mass down her back, she closes her eyes and sits there motionless. Something unendurable seems to be taking possession of her soul. She suddenly cannot remember why she has come, what it is she wants. How frightening! Perhaps she will remember ... and as though recalling why, she unconsciously runs her hands through her hair....

Is she conscious of the sounds around her?

No.

Her mind swims with thoughts of Mavra, Hryts, fern blossoms and St. John's Eve, and the evil that is hidden in Hryts which she must destroy.... Finally she becomes confused, but continues to tug at her long, silken hair.

But what is this? She lifts her head and her dark brows. Had she not heard this before now? It is a man's voice in Mavra's cottage. She strains to hear what is being said. Listening, she seems to come to her senses and then grows paler and paler.

She hears the same voice that gave her the news that Hryts is marrying Nastia, that he loved both of them. He is telling Mavra that the two of them should not go and confess to Hryts whose son he is, because he does not like gypsies, and it might even turn his foster parents against him if they find out he is the son of a poor gypsy woman and the grandson of a gypsy. It would be better to wait until after the wedding next week to tell him everything. Tetiana again lost her composure. Hearing again about the wedding of Hryts and Nastia, she uttered a strange cry and leaped up from her place. And when Mavra, summoned by the frenzied cry, appeared on the threshold with Andronati on her heels, she had already disappeared into the forest.

That terrible old man who seemed to have come up from hell, that very same one, was repeating the same things! Again about Hryts and Nastia. Oh-h-h! Again, and again, and again!... Something is happening to her, she does not know what. She ran until her strength gave out, scrambling up the mountainside, then dropping weakly to the ground, realizing that she is at the White Rock. Yes, this is where she used to meet with Hryts and he will be here soon.

"Hryts, I'm here!" She called out in a far-reaching, enticing voice, and waited. She did not wait long. A new thought came to disturb her. Will he come? And right after that another. Who is to blame? Blue-eyed Nastia? Oh no! Nastia is not to blame. Is Hryts to blame? No, she loves him and he is not to blame for anything. Not he. It is the evil that caused it all. *Evil has hidden itself in him* so that no one can find it. It keeps Hryts from meeting her, it has killed her happiness. *It* is to blame. She will destroy it. She found it in Hryts and she will destroy it in him. Yes, in him. She will go to Hryts now and destroy it in him. Yes, in him. She will go to Hryts now and tell him everything. Let him know, too. She will go to Hryts ... and lifting herself up from the ground, her wide, staring eyes fell on the broad-leafed herbs growing beneath the White Rock.

"Hey, what a lot of it is here! The place is full of it. Hey, Mavra," she calls out breathlessly in wild rapture. "There are a lot of your herbs growing here! Ah, Mavra!" Her earlier thoughts about the old gypsy woman flooded her mind and she was again confused. What had Mavra said about the herb growing beneath the White Rock? She thinks for a moment. Now she remembers. *It is good for all things evil*, instructed Mavra. "*On Sunday morning,*" she had said, "*gather the herbs, on Monday rinse them, on Tuesday cook them, and on Wednesday....* On Wednesday?" Her thoughts seethe and cannot find an answer....

She sat down again beside the plants and reflected, her dark brows arched in perplexity. On Wednesday?—Mavra had said something about Wednesday. Ah, now she remembers. On Wednesday, Mavra said, *you lull the evil to sleep.* And the wedding is on Sunday!

Yes. The old man said the wedding is on Sunday. With that she looks again at the herb. There is a lot of it. It reaches out to one's hands by itself, begging to be gathered. Mavra will be glad, *and she herself will kill the evil hidden in Hryts.* But quickly—quickly—so it won't get away.... With her fingers trembling convulsively and with frenzied speed, as though someone were standing there urging her on, Tetiana digs and tears at the herb, gathering it up in her apron. Having picked more than enough, she stands up, and throwing her head back until her hair almost touches the ground, cries out with all her might: "I will come!"—and immediately after, her voice imitating a lark, she cries again, happily, ~~"I love!"~~ Silent now, her huge eyes staring far into the distance, her dark brows arching, she listens: from the opposite mountain, as though it has just reached it, comes the echo from across the ravine:

"I love!"

* * *

It is Wednesday evening before the wedding.

Mavra stands beside her bench sorting out herbs by candlelight, deliberating about which to give Tetiana to relieve her grief over Hryts. Today she had gone to see Ivanykha Dub whose hair has turned gray from grief during this short period of time.

She has finished sorting them out. She will give Tetiana the herbs growing beneath the White Rock. It is a good, wonder-working herb. A small amount puts one to sleep—like a magic formula it quiets the heart and mind; but too great a dose sometimes causes death.

No, her reflections suddenly stop, she cannot give Tetiana the herbs today. It is too late, and besides, Tetiana is not at home. Perhaps tomorrow. The unfortunate girl has wandered the forest for three days now. People have even seen her in the neighbouring village where she had spent the night. Besides, her father Andronati had promised to visit her tonight. She expects him any moment now, so she cannot leave the house. Such were Mavra's ruminations while she sorted and separated her herbs.

In all these mountains that tower here, there is no one happier than Mavra. She has found her father whom she thought dead and now knows that Hryts from the Hungarian border, the foster son of Mykhailo Donchuk, is her son, who was stolen from her. On learning all this she became almost hysterical in her happiness. She, a poor, useless gypsy, alone on the entire mountain, in the entire forest, is the mother of a handsome young man, and her father, Andronati, is alive. He had come to her here. He had accidentally learned from Hryts and Nastia that a gypsy fortune-teller lives all alone on Chabanytsia Mountain and had sought her out at once.

Lord! She had cried out of misery, out of hardship, worry, grief, and sadness, but she had cried with joy when her father stepped over her threshold and they had recognized each other. He had barely recognized her, she had aged so much, and she was frightened at seeing his long, grey beard and bent shoulders. Then the regrets crept in. He had already been here beside her house, during the past cold winter. He had begged and prayed to be let in, and she had not opened the door. They would have recognized each other then, and he, bent and grey, could have lived with her, he would not have had to return to Hungary in the cold of winter. Mavra repented, crying bitterly. And then her cards told her that two men would visit her house.

An old man and a young one. Happiness with one and grief with the other.

"Happiness with you, father," she said immediately. "Happiness with you, but grief with whom?"

Had any other man been to see her, the old man asked, since the time she had refused him entry to her house? Try to remember, he said, think.

She thought and pondered, then remembered. There was only one other one—the handsome, proud young man on the black horse. She had also read his cards, sought his destiny. She had warned him not to love two and foretold a long journey; he would know good fortune, but would lose it on this journey. She had not told him that, of course. He had paid her handsomely....

While she was telling this story, Andronati listened with a gleam in his eyes.

Had she asked him his name?

No, she had not. She only knew that he had made her feel sorry for him. He was so like the one whom she, a sinner, had loved and through him had ruined her life. Young and handsome he was, and he looked exactly like that one.

Her father then told her what he had done in order to save her life, which Radu was preparing to take; how he had given the entire clan a drink containing herbs, and her, too, so he could take her out of the camp. Thank God that he had been successful. As for the child, he had left it on the doorstep of a wealthy family so that Radu would not kill it, so it would not die beside her in the forest, but find a better fate than that of a gypsy... He hoped that Mavra would not perish, would find a shelter among good people, and that one day he would find her. He had not told his grandson his gypsy background so as not to spoil his prospects. He came into the area only from time to time to reassure himself that he was living well. He was now convinced that he had done the right thing in leaving him on the doorstep, for he had landed in good hands. Now, as a great favour he begged her not to tell him about his background yet, not until his foster-father gives him some land, until he becomes a property owner in his own right. His foster parents are wealthy landowners, very proud. If they learned of his background too soon, they might even throw his grandfather and mother out of their home and refuse to give the lad a parcel of land. Let her wait, keep quiet like him in the meantime, and all will work out well for them and the boy. He had kept quiet as a stone all these years and see how well things were turning out. Hryts will be getting married soon, go out on his own, and his young wife, a fine, fair girl, also well-off, has promised that they will take him, an old man, to live with them. He has done her a favour and is counting on her promise in this. Once he settles in with them, Hryts will not disown his mother. So she must not say anything to spoil the boy's future. They will go to the wedding, he has invited them both, and there ... just wait. When the time is ripe, they will talk. Mavra resisted and cried. She was eager to acknowledge her son. But Andronati scolded and cursed and even, according to his habit, struck her a few times in his fury. Only then did Mavra submit to his advice and agreed to follow it.

Only one thing clouds her happiness, one thing oppresses and chokes her—Tetiana's grief caused by her son and the pain suffered by the good Ivanykha Dub. Why did Hryts not love Tetiana to the end? *The end?* She asked herself this question a hundred times. What a turn this whole affair would have taken for them, her poor mother and her, too! My son, why did you so sunder your soul? And she, too, has contributed to Tetiana's grief by telling his fortune, warning him to beware of dark eyes...

Her worry and pity for Tetiana give her no rest, take away her appetite. The girl is probably ruined for life. Who knows or can say whether Tetiana will ever fully return to what she had been. There are times when it seems she has returned to normal, Ivanykha Dub told her, and other times when she is quite mad, she does not recognize anyone, will not see anyone, and always talks about Hryts and *evil*. How will it all end? O Lord, why is it so difficult for people to find happiness? For her, too. She has found her son, but is losing Tetiana. She barely knows who is closer to her heart, her son or Tetiana? One is getting married and the other is left heartbroken, without a future....

Why had Tetiana not confided in her? Immediately, right from the very beginning. Why was she so secretive, not even letting her mother know of their meetings? How can the situation be saved now? How can this disaster be eliminated? This terrible disaster! Thinking of the ruination of the beautiful young girl by her own child—her son—Mavra wept.

Then she smiled bitterly. How like his father he was! He has two souls. He clung to Nastia and loved Tetiana. If only Tetiana had admitted it all in the beginning.... Hm.... *If only*! If only she had known *then* that her son was alive. Then! But her father.... Here her thoughts broke off. She is to blame, only she. Her father had long ago begged and implored her to let him into her home and she had refused him shelter. He must have put a curse on her then. And he could evoke terrible curses. Did he not curse her happiness then, sentencing her to a life of grief?

Neither Hryts nor Tetiana are to blame here, but who—who, then, is to blame? Mavra asks herself in tears. Hryts, my son, why did you have to take after your father? Why not your mother ... and here, as earlier, her thoughts broke off. Was she, his mother, any *better*? She had a husband and betrayed him. Oh-h-h! She groaned suddenly, beating at her head with her fists. "Sin, sin, sin" wept her heart. A great terrible sin without end. The *sin* is to blame for everything, the sin alone!...

But she will save Tetiana. Let be what will be. She will save Tetiana. At least until Sunday, at least till after the wedding, she will make it her task to bring her back to her senses, return her to reason. She will go out early, on Sunday at dawn, to the White Rock, dig up some herbs and try. First she will induce sleep with these herbs, then with sorcery, and after seven weeks of supplication to the new moon, she will calm down. In time she will forget Hryts and marry another.

So Mavra thinks and ponders while sorting and putting her various herbs in order, each according to its purpose, when suddenly she is startled by a knock at her door.

Who can it be at this late hour? It is already long past midnight. She had not gone to bed, because she was expecting her father. He had gone for alms to a neighbouring town and she, with her distressing thoughts and her herbs had delayed her sleep.

Can this be Tetiana?

"Who is it?" she calls out cautiously, from habit.

"It is I," a voice answers.

"Tetiana?" asks Mavra, listening closely. Perhaps it is the unfortunate girl who is wandering the forest and has reached her house, attracted by her light.

"No, it is I," answers the same voice.

Mavra opens the door.

A girl stood before her. She is tall, young and fair of face, her eyes swollen with weeping.

Mavra looks at her with interest that turns to discomfort.

"What is it, daughter, at such a late hour? It's well past midnight. But sit down right here. Your eyes are weeping. Is your heart weeping, too? Those with an aching heart should come to Mavra," she says, as if in prayer, but her gleaming eyes pierce the girl inquisitively.

"Help me, Mother!" cries the girl, sinking down to the bench. "My betrothed is ill, maybe even dying. He talks in his sleep. No one understands what he is saying. Help, Mother!" she wept. Sinking to her knees, she lifts her arms despairingly and prays: "O Lord of the heavens—how have I offended you? Why are you punishing me? I am not guilty of anything. I loved him truly, body and soul. It was she ... she!" she cried bitterly.

"Hush, daughter, hush now," Mavra soothed the girl and helps her to rise. "Tell me what is wrong with your betrothed, whose child you are, and if I can, I will help. I won't leave you in your distress."

"I am Nastia, Hryts's betrothed," cries the girl and again extends her arms to Mavra, beseeching her. "*Someone has laid a spell on him*. He had his breakfast this morning, then fell asleep and has been sleeping ever since, a completely lifeless sleep. At first he was talking, muttering that someone was coming, that he will *come* soon, then he stopped...."

"You are Hryts's betrothed?" Mavra shouted, tugging at the girl like a madwoman.

"Yes, I am. I'm his betrothed, Mother, and Sunday is our wedding day."

"Hryts!" Mavra cried out in a terrible voice and sank to the ground. "Son! My son! He is dying, he is departing just when I have found him! Wait for your mother, Hryts, she is coming. Wait, don't die!" Her last words, evoked by some inhuman strength, revitalized her as never before. She leaped to her feet, swept up her bundle of herbs, grabbed the girl by the hand and the two of them rushed out of the house.

Breathing heavily and groaning, old Mavra rushes along the mountainside against the wind as though on wings, with Nastia running after, barely keeping on her feet. Only one thing sustains her—her complete faith in Mavra's powers, without that she would be powerless.

"He is under a spell. He has been poisoned!" she shouts after Mavra. "A bottle was found beneath the window. Our shepherd saw a girl running through the forest, some girl *with black brows*...."

"Tetiana!" screams Mavra and halts. She turns cold and crosses herself. "This is what sin brings—what it brings," she groans and slows her pace—she has no more strength left.

It was Thursday morning when they reached the house, and when they arrived, it was all over. Hryts had left this world.

* * *

There was solemnity and sorrow by Hryts's home.

His foster parents and everyone who knew Hryts had gathered to mourn. They were bowed down in their sorrow and silently waited. The fair Nastia swoons in her home, the women weep. His friends, the young lads of the village, walk around and wipe their tears. The mothers, speaking in hushed whispers, cross themselves and pray.

A bitter and exhausting scene had just taken place in front of the house. The gypsy Mavra, in unheard-of despair, had thrown herself like a she-wolf at her father. He had taken her son from her, she wailed, taken him and left him to landowners so that he would have a better life, and look at the fate that he met in his abundances....

No one had ever heard such lamentations, seen such behaviour as that of the poor gypsy woman. She threw herself face down on the ground, tore at her clothes, stretched her arms to the sky in despairing prayers, spoke without stopping until her strength left her.

Old Andronati defended himself at first—then was silent.

Propping himself with all the weight of his aged body on his beggar's staff, he stood silent. He did not even notice that after his grieving daughter had stopped lamenting, he had begun to listen to the sorrowful wails of the Trembita sounding over the mountain above the house.

With its sadness it reminded him of something far in the past. Long, long ago it had also wailed as sorrowfully, he recalled.

He had stood that morning at sunrise, high on the mountain over this village, holding his white grandchild in his arms. Holding him thus, he had searched the blue morning mist for the child's destiny. The mist was not rising. He had not seen it then through the mist-covered sun, but it was there. His grandson *had* a future. It was only awaiting him, like that morning sun behind the mist—why had he not reached it?

* * *

Among those present in the house is Ivanykha Dub.

She is waiting for Tetiana. Maybe she will at least show herself here. She is not at home—no one has seen her. She is roaming the forests, avoiding people.

Having arrived here, Ivanykha Dub was struck speechless. No one hears a single word from her, it is as though she has forgotten how to talk. She merely pushes her grey hair under her black kerchief from time to time with a shaking hand. She waits.

Will her waiting be in vain?

Perhaps not.

The people stare at her, whispering. She pays no heed. Her eyes are dry, her lips pressed together, only her soul is slowly petrifying.

There is a rustle at the door. Her Tetiana? No, it is Mavra with her father, coming in to look at her son. But what is this? Son of God! Through the windows from outside the house comes a song—quavering, unearthly. Ivanykha Dub pales and sags; it is Tetiana.

Yes. It is Tetiana.

Tall, emaciated, pale, her dishevelled hair adorned with poppies, her eyes unseeing—it is *she*.

No one moves.

She enters, her dark brows arched, her finger to her lips as if requesting silence, then begins to speak in a sing-song voice:

"*On Sunday morning I gathered herbs, on Monday morning I rinsed them ...* hush Mavra," she adds pleadingly, "*and on Tuesday,* Mavra," she adds, her eyes half-closed as if trying to remember, "*I boiled the herbs, and on Wednesday morning...,*" she pauses.... "Hush, Mavra," she beseeches with deep tenderness and a far-away look, "hush. I have killed the *evil ... with your herbs*, Mavra, from beneath the White Rock. He will sleep it off. Hush! The wedding is on Sunday. Hush!" She stops, waits a moment, dropping her head back on her shoulders as if from deep exhaustion, and closes her eyes.

Everyone was stunned.

No, not everyone. Silently, like an uncoiling serpent, Mavra moves toward her.

"*Bitch!*" she screamed savagely. "You have poisoned my son! You, you, you! Die!" And with a mighty blow of her fist she knocks the girl to the floor. But here Ivanykha Dub appears at her daughter's side.

"Stop!" she shouted, while everyone quaked. "Kill *me* while you're at it. She is ready. Now *finish* me off!"

Then raising her daughter, who was convulsively clutching at the flowers in her hair, to her feet, she asked through pale lips:

"My beloved child, my one and only in the world—*you* poisoned Hryts?"

Tetiana smiles.

"Hush, Mavra!" she whispers, her dark brows arched. "Evil was hidden in
him.... Hush! There'll be no more evil now, anywhere...."

"Daughter!" Again with a superhuman effort her mother beseeches,
holding her daughter tenderly, like a small child. "You? Tell everyone the
truth. Was it you? Say it as though to the Lord...."

Tetiana looks long into her mother's eyes as if trying to recall something,
then cuddling up to her mother's breast with the genuine affection of a child
and clutching convulsively at her flowers like before, she begins to sing
tenderly and softly, as if she were telling a secret:

> Hey, on St. John's Eve, hey on Kupala's Eve.... Hey, hey, hey!...
> A beautiful maiden her fortune sought—hey, hey, hey!

On the final word she suddenly tears herself from her mother's arms and
speeds like an arrow out of the house. Silently, without a single word,
Ivanykha Dub topples to the ground.

* * *

They buried Hryts, and the people dispersed.

"Come, Mavra," said old Andronati to his daughter when it was all over.
"Let us go to the gypsies. Now we are old people here once again."

"Let's go, father," Mavra says firmly, giving her father his long staff. "My
sin has ended here."

And so they went.

The firs and the pines sway lightly and brush against them, as they often
did when they would walk along the White Path, and the murmur of the forest
sways, soothing the broken strings in their souls until they leave the forest,
and when they had left it behind, it disappeared completely, and night crept
slowly over the forest.

* * *

Ivanykha Dub, together with the villagers, searched the entire forest and
all its hiding places where Tetiana was wont to wander, but did not find
her. She had disappeared without a trace. It was already midnight, but

Ivanykha Dub is lying exhausted and debilitated in her bed, straining at every sound. Her heart tells her that Tetiana will return now that it is midnight. There, she hears a rustle. Tetiana will return on her own, as she always has. Dawn is not far away. If only it were already here! Once she returns she will take her to a nunnery and put her into God's hands. Only God can make her whole again, give her strength. Only God, and then it will be as God wills it.

It is quiet in the house, like a sanctuary, only the sputtering of the lighted candle before the icon of the Blessed Virgin Mary can be heard. Ivanykha Dub waits, listening, her closed eyes brimming over with tears.

There—another rustle. No, it is the river. It is never silent. She wakes a number of times from a half-sleep. The river irritates her, it seems to be demanding something.

Suddenly—and now she is not mistaken. She hears something clearly, but cannot distinguish what it is. Is it the humming of bees, the delicate strumming of strings, or the voices of angels? She cannot tell. But she hears something, she is not mistaken.

Into her ears flows a wondrously soft, melodious voice, light as a dream, like the hum of bees, like silk drawn across strings, lifting her soul into the celestial clouds:

> Hey, on St. John's Eve, hey on Kupala's Eve…. Hey, hey, hey!…
> A beautiful maiden her fortune sought—hey, hey, hey!

Ivanykha Dub starts up. God Almighty, it is Tetiana! Yes, it was Tetiana's voice. She heard it clearly. It is her beloved voice. She is singing outside the window, searching for the door.

Ivanykha Dub rises quickly. She hurries, staggering to the door, opens it and looks….

She must have been dreaming. Outside it was broad daylight with a smiling sun lighting up everything brightly—but no Tetiana. Ivanykha Dub broke out in a cold sweat. Had she only dreamt Tetiana's singing? Had she really heard it? A terrible thought suddenly flashed into her mind and she sped to the servants.

They all head for the river, to search there as well, hoping to find at least some trace of her there.

They went.

They did not walk for long.

There, where the depths held sway, where the giant boulder quietly marked the motionless deepth of the river, where Tetiana's wreath had once sunk to the bottom, one large red poppy was nestling against the rock. The other, perched by the riverbank, waited, and like the other, was not moving...

Ivanykha Dub stands and gazes at the two blossoms, mute with shock, all the servants at her side.

For a long time she gazes at them, then turns her back on them.

Ivanykha Dub was led away.

Chernivtsi, April 1908.

Translated by Mary Skrypnyk